# Coleridge's

# Metaphors of Being

*Princeton*
*Essays in Literature*

FOR A COMPLETE LIST
OF TITLES,
SEE PAGES 203 & 204

# Coleridge's

# Metaphors of Being

## EDWARD KESSLER

PRINCETON UNIVERSITY PRESS

PRINCETON, NEW JERSEY

Copyright © 1979 by Princeton University Press
Published by Princeton University Press, Princeton, New Jersey
In the United Kingdom: Princeton University Press, Guildford,
Surrey

All Rights Reserved
Library of Congress Cataloging in Publication Data will be
found on the last printed page of this book

Publication of this book has been aided by a grant from The
Andrew W. Mellon Foundation

This book has been composed in Linotype Janson

Clothbound editions of Princeton University Press books
are printed on acid-free paper, and binding materials are
chosen for strength and durability

Printed in the United States of America by Princeton
University Press, Princeton, New Jersey

*For John Ciardi*

# Contents

Acknowledgments                                          ix

Abbreviations of Works by Coleridge                       x

Introduction                                              3

1. The Eddy-Rose                                         15

2. Phantom                                               39

3. Limbo                                                 83

4. Beyond Metaphor:
   Coleridge's Abstract Self                            123

5. Afterword: Journey of Two Magi                       185

Works Cited                                             195

Index                                                  199

# Acknowledgments

ACKNOWLEDGMENTS are due to the Princeton University Press for permission to quote from the published volumes of Coleridge's *Notebooks*, particularly volumes II and III, from which I have reproduced extensive sections, the original manuscript versions of the poems "Coeli Enarrant," "Limbo," and "Ne Plus Ultra." I have also transcribed some other entries. Professor Kathleen Coburn's extraordinary scholarly labors have made my commentary possible. The Oxford University Press has granted me permission to quote from the standard *Complete Poetical Works of Samuel Taylor Coleridge* as well as from Coleridge's *Collected Letters*.

I wish to thank Walter Jackson Bate for encouraging me at the initial stage of my research, and George Whalley for reading an early portion of the book and offering substantial criticism. Two thoughtful readers of the text in its completed form saved me from considerable error: Richard Harter Fogle and J. Robert Barth, S.J. Several colleagues helped by reading and commenting along the way: Rudolph von Abele, C. Barry Chabot, Jeanne Addison Roberts, and Marion Trousdale. From a seminar on Coleridge, two student papers influenced my interpretation of certain poems: I thank Nancy Goodley and Richard Kinsey. And Anne Waring Warren generously provided books that made the job much easier.

Other friends have helped make the voyage on Coleridge's wide wide sea less lonely. In London: Betty Bostetter, Marion Trousdale, Bart Winer, and George Whalley. In Boston: Avis DeVoto, James Harrington, and Sally Portle. I particularly want to thank John Malcolm Brinnin for allowing me to use his office at Boston University during the course of two summers.

# Abbreviations of Works by Coleridge

AP      *Anima Poetae*. Ed. E. H. Coleridge (from the *Notebooks*). London. 1895.

AR      *Aids to Reflection*. Ed. H. N. Coleridge. London. 1825.

BL      *Biographia Literaria*. Ed. J. Shawcross. 2 vols. Oxford. 1962.

CC      *The Collected Works of Samuel Taylor Coleridge*. Ed. Kathleen Coburn and Bart Winer. Princeton. 1969—.

CIS      *Confessions of an Inquiring Spirit*. Ed. H. N. Coleridge. London. 1849.

CL      *Collected Letters of Samuel Taylor Coleridge*. Ed. E. L. Griggs. 6 vols. Oxford. 1956-1971.

CN      *The Notebooks of Samuel Taylor Coleridge*. Ed. Kathleen Coburn. Princeton. 1957—.

*Friend*      *The Friend*. Ed. Barbara E. Rooke. 2 vols. (CC IV). 1969.

LR      *The Literary Remains*. Ed. H. N. Coleridge. 4 vols. London. 1836-1839.

LS      *Lay Sermons*. Ed. R. J. White. (CC VI). 1972.

MC      *Miscellaneous Criticism*. Ed. Thomas Middleton Raysor. Cambridge, Mass. 1936.

PL      *The Philosophical Lectures*. Ed. Kathleen Coburn. London. 1949.

PW      *The Complete Poetical Works of Samuel Taylor Coleridge*. Ed. E. H. Coleridge. 2 vols. Oxford. 1912.

Shedd   *The Complete Works of Samuel Taylor Coleridge.* Ed. W.G.T. Shedd. 7 vols. New York. 1856.

ShC     *Coleridge's Shakespearean Criticism.* Ed. T. M. Raysor. 2 vols. Cambridge, Mass. 1930.

TL      *Hints Toward the Formation of a More Comprehensive Theory of Life.* Ed. Seth B. Watson. London. 1848.

TM      *Treatise on Method.* Ed. Alice D. Snyder. London. 1934.

TT      *Specimens of the Table Talk of the Late S. T. Coleridge.* Ed. H. N. Coleridge. 2 vols. London. 1835.

*Coleridge's*

*Metaphors of Being*

# Introduction

THIS essay grew out of an interest in Coleridge's later poems, particularly "Limbo," and out of a feeling that Coleridge was not the failed poet he claimed to be. At twenty-one he was lamenting, "I am but the Dregs of my former self" (CL,I,47), and by the year 1800 (at twenty-eight) he had given up entirely: "As to Poetry, I have altogether abandoned it, being convinced that I never had the essentials of poetic Genius, & that I mistook a strong desire for original power" (CL,I,656). Taking him at his word, Coleridge's contemporaries and most subsequent critics have explored the reasons for his failure or shifted their attention to his prose: his literary criticism, and his philosophical and religious writings. It is assumed that Coleridge's standards of excellence were so high and his self-confidence so low, that after his few great poems he became an artist without an art, dwelling on some middle ground, pursuing his "abstruse research," occasionally turning out a few "trifles and fragments." Wordsworth, soon after Coleridge's death, could possibly have been describing his friend's poetic life:

> Nor has the rolling year twice measured,
> From sign to sign, its steadfast course,
> Since every mortal power of Coleridge
> Was frozen at its marvellous source. . . .[1]

I hope to show that Coleridge's source was never frozen, and that his poetic stream, "meandering with a mazy motion," sometimes sinking beneath a dry surface or emerging

[1] William Wordsworth, "Extempore Effusion upon the Death of James Hogg," *The Poetical Works of William Wordsworth*, ed. E. de Selincourt and Helen Darbishire (Oxford: Clarendon Press, 1947), IV, 277.

3

"momently" as a fountain, was continuously present. In the midst of his analysis of Coleridge's religious thought in the late *Aids to Reflection*, Basil Willey parenthetically interjects: "(Yes! let us not forget, as in a study of this kind we too easily may, that it is a *poet* we have to deal with)."[2] I would like to help release the poet from that parenthesis.

Denying himself the honorific title of poet, Coleridge proceeded to create a "poetry of Being" that could appear in prose as well as in poems, in sustained discourse or as momentary fragments or *aperçus*. His energy was not diverted from poetry, but was spent in bringing poetry into the service of Being, in making it follow the "working of the mind," regardless of whether the result was made visible as a conventional poetic form, a finished product. In *The Examiner* of 1816, Hazlitt attacked Coleridge in a most vulnerable spot: "the fault of Mr. Coleridge is, that he comes to no conclusion. He is a man of that universality of genius, that his mind hangs suspended between poetry and prose."[3] Precisely because Coleridge's idea of Being resisted definition, his poetic impulse resisted conclusions, even a conclusive distinction between poetry and prose.[4] The

[2] Basil Willey, *Samuel Taylor Coleridge* (New York: W. W. Norton & Co., 1973), p. 234.

[3] Quoted in *Coleridge: The Critical Heritage*, ed. J. R. de J. Jackson (London: Routledge & Kegan Paul, 1970), p. 205.

[4] As a critic, Coleridge labored to make a clear distinction between a "poem" and prose, but often "poetry" appears disguised in notebook entries and other prose writing. In a remarkable letter (CL,II,714), the poet creates what I see as a moving "modern" poem: "—You would not know me—! all sounds of similitude keep at such a distance from each other in my mind, that I have *forgotten* how to make a rhyme—I look at the Mountains (that visible God Almighty that looks in at all my windows) I look at the Mountains only for the Curves of their outlines; the Stars, as I behold them, form themselves into Triangles—and my hands are scarred with scratches from a Cat, whose back I was rubbing in the Dark in order to see whether the sparks from it were refrangible by a Prism. The Poet is dead in me—my imagination (or rather the Somewhat that had been imaginative) lies, like a Cold Snuff on the circular Rim of a Brass Candle-stick, without even a stink of Tallow to remind

4

finite form of Being, or of a poem, remains something to be *seen through*: "the finite form can neither be laid hold of, nor is it any thing of itself real, but merely an apprehension, a frame-work which the human imagination forms by its own limits, as the foot measures itself on the snow" (*Friend*,I,520). Many of Coleridge's late poems are fragments, footprints on the snow, that point toward a conception of Being that is metaphysical. What at first may appear as the inability to conclude can be viewed as a deliberate (if not fully acknowledged) act of rejecting the limitations of what the poet called "confining form." He may have remained, as Professor Bate says, "probably the most conservative of all English poets," but he was surely aware that he was venturing into uncharted poetic territory. In the 1828 edition of his poems, the section including "Duty Surviving Self-Love," "Phantom or Fact," "Youth and Age," "The Blossoming of the Solitary Date-Tree," and other late poems, is headed:

Prose in Rhyme
or,
Epigrams, Moralities, and Things
Without a Name.

He consistently avoided calling most of his works "poems,"[5] and his motive is not entirely explained by The Anxiety of Influence or The Burden of the Past. The end of the poetic process was not a poem (as an artifact), but a new knowl-

---

you that it was once cloathed & mitred with Flame. That is past by! —I was once a Volume of Gold Leaf, rising & riding on every breath of Fancy—but I have beaten myself back into weight & density, & now I sink in quicksilver, yea, remain squat and square on the earth amid the hurricane, that makes Oaks and Straws join in one Dance, fifty yards high in the Element."

[5] Besides "thoughts punctuated by rhymes" and "that which effects not to be poetry," Coleridge's list of substitutes for "poem" includes lines (or verses or stanzas), effusions, vision, epistles, fragments, improvisation, translation, imitation, "a Desultory poem," and "a poem it ought to be."

edge of the self, a new awareness of Being. The modern prose poem, free verse, and the fragment as a form may all have had their beginnings in Coleridge's "failure."

I hope that Coleridge's personal definition of Being will emerge from his own writing and my commentary, but perhaps a few preliminary remarks will tentatively ground the term that Heidegger, in our own day, relentlessly labored to authenticate. For Coleridge, Being is a process, a coming into Being; and like the meaning of a poem, it is revealed through acts, not objects. Being is the energy shining through phenomena, a movement toward that "ultimate Being" which cannot finally be realized in time and space. Perhaps his purest evocation of Being in poetry appeared in these "lines," which will be discussed below:

> All look and likeness caught from earth,
> All accident of kin and birth,
> Had pass'd away. There was no trace
> Of aught on that illumined face,
> Uprais'd beneath the rifted stone
> But of one spirit all her own;—
> She, she herself, and only she,
> Shone through her body visibly.

(PW,I,393)

To make his own Being visible was the task he assumed in his later years, and poetry became his means but not his end. Unlike Heidegger, Coleridge denied Being-Toward-Death because death was no fact for the poet: it ends bodily existence but not life. Even in his darkest moments, when he despaired of achieving salvation, he believed in a *telos* outside space and time, an absolute, a meaning that provides the end for man's spiritual evolution. A completed life or a completed poem was disturbing to him. He viewed Being as a perpetual joining together of what we are and what we can be.

Heidegger and Coleridge were both concerned with confronting the Mystery of Being, the hidden reality that may find its temporary accommodation in language, which Heidegger called "Being's House." The philosopher and the poet found themselves ever on the "threshold," in Coleridge's "Limbo," and consequently suffered anxiety, doubt, and the pangs of being an outsider. Moreover, both demanded of themselves a profound personal engagement, rejecting the common escapes offered by abstract thoughts without a thinker, or physical acts that are merely object-oriented. Man must risk himself in order to find himself; and like the Ancient Mariner, he must enter the abyss and endure isolation and loneliness before he can begin to discover what lies on the other side. But whereas Heidegger revealed Being in the world, without depending on metaphysics, Coleridge aspired to make his Being independent of phenomena—and of traditional forms of poetry as phenomena. Man's "natural knowledge" had finally to be subordinated to a new system, "the first principle of which it is to render the mind intuitive of the *spiritual* in man (i.e. of that which lies *on the other side* of our natural consciousness) must have a greater obscurity for those, who have never disciplined and strengthened their ulterior consciousness" (BL,i,168). Because Coleridge was a Christian both in and out of time, he could never give Being and Time equal status, united by a neutral copula. The world is never enough, neither is the phenomenal self: "I adore the living and personal God, whose Power indeed is the *Ground* of all Being . . . but who may not without fearful error be identified with the universe, or the universe be considered as an *attribute* of his Deity" (CL,iv,894).

Perhaps the greatest single difference between Coleridge and Heidegger is found in the philosopher's self-sufficiency and the poet's constant need for something outside the self to bring about even a momentary apprehension of Being. Coleridge's search for an originating voice—not his own voice echoing from external nature—was continually thwarted during his lifetime, but he never consciously withdrew into self-isolation to become, like Heidegger, the

7

preserver of a past order. His constancy was always toward the *other*, whether it appear as another human being, his own ideal self, or the personal God who so often remained silent. God may know himself without external manifestation, but human beings can evolve their "ulterior consciousness" only by joining in a process: "I mean that *willing* sense of the insufficingness of the *self* for itself, which predisposes a generous nature to see, in the total being of another, the supplement and completion of its own;—that quiet perpetual *seeking* which the presence of the beloved object modulates, not suspends, where the heart momently finds, and, finding, again seeks on" (PW,I,465). Coleridge was a "subject" who required the modulating power of love objects; his continual seeking and finding indicate that Being cannot illuminate itself in isolation. The poet's worst fears occurred when he thought he would never find his "supplement and completion," and would remain an arrested Being, a realized object instead of a self-realizing subject.

As Coleridge moved into his later years, traditional metaphor, "a mere metaphor, or conventional exponent of a thing," (LR,III,110) became inadequate as a means of expressing a Being that was steadily moving beyond the world's appearances. Metaphor, by its very nature, locates the poet in the physical world, and it became less and less effective in furthering an evolution that was taking place within the consciousness. The poetic image as a representation could only re-present the already known; it was of questionable aid in creating a new self, the Being about to be. Thoughts, not things, are the objects of the mind, and Coleridge believed that the greatest minds do not depend on the world to reflect them and "rest content between thought and reality, as it were in an intermundium of which their own living spirit supplies the *substance*, and their imagination the ever-varying *form*" (BL,I,20). If Being was to emerge from its "house" in nature and language, Coleridge needed a new personal form to declare it, without restricting it within earthly boundaries. Both physical and spiritual evolution, continuously seeking an end, would be *mis*represented by any fixed thought or thing, any inherited shape. The poem as icon had to be shattered; the current of life had to be interrupted momentarily so that Being could be apprehended. The fragment was Coleridge's form for Being-in-Time, and symbol and paradox became his means of conveying a sense of form. Alert to the danger of "the understanding of Metaphor for Reality" (CN,II,2711),[6] Coleridge knew that he was demanding a great deal from those readers not developed enough to enter his "intermundium," where phantoms and facts come together and are not clearly distinguishable: "for such men it is either literal or metaphorical. There is no third. For to the *Symbolical* they have not arrived" (CL,v,91). (The symbol, in the poet's well-known definition, "partakes of the reality it renders intelligible.") In attempting to remake poetic form, Coleridge was attempting to remake himself, and in breaking from natural and metaphorical form he was compelled to sacrifice his former harmony with his surroundings. He aspired to create "a form that all informs against/itself" (CN,II,2921), and his personal alienation, his despair, his vacant moods—what he called his "negative Being"—was an essential opposite: the fragment could point toward the wholeness, fullness, and coherence that only characterize *ultimate* Being. The stone had to be "rifted" before Being could emerge: the stone of language and self.

Quite early in life Coleridge began suffering the anxiety that was to pervade his later poems: that doubt and "negative Being" which he came to see as a necessary stage in his spiritual growth. Like an organism, he needed to divide in order to recreate himself. He needed to experience poverty before he could know the luxury of Being. He wrote in 1798 some words that profoundly apply to his later poems: "I have, at times, experienced such an extinction of *Light*

---

[6] Later, Coleridge warned his readers of the possibility that spiritual mystery "will be evaporated into metaphors" (AR,294).

in my mind, I have been so forsaken by all the *forms* and *colourings* of Existence, as if the *organs* of Life had been dried up; as if only simple *Being* remained, blind and stagnant!" (CL,I,470). This experience foreshadows those lonely, abandoned figures that populate the later poems and represent the poet who cannot will his own spiritual history. Coleridge recognized in Shakespeare the consummate artist who "projected his mind out of his own particular being" until he became the object of his meditation (CN,III,3290). But Coleridge's defective will became the *matter* for his own meditation; by exposing his own self-indulgence he hoped to make way for self-realization. Before he could outgrow the world, his own shadow standing between himself and the light, he had to endure "no Sun, no Light with vivifying Warmth, but a cold and dull moonshine, or rather star-light, which shews itself but shews nothing else" (CL,II,1196). The poet, out of his own fragmented self, created an art that shows more than itself, one that reveals Being.

In the title of this essay, "Metaphors of Being," I have tried to indicate Coleridge's desire to reach beyond conventional metaphor, natural representation or picture language, into the mystery of Being. The "of" provides the possibility of a dual reading that is singularly appropriate to Coleridge's uncertainty and self-division. The Metaphors belong to Being, are a part of Being and are hence symbolic. But, on the other hand, they are only signs for Being and must be interpreted by a sympathetic reader before their meaning can be disclosed. As the poet wrote: "Every Book worthy of being read at all must be read in and by the same Spirit, as that by which it was written. Who does not do this, reads a Sun Dial by moonshine."[7] As he progressed, Coleridge moved inevitably into abstraction, away from "all look and likeness caught from earth/ All accident of kin and birth," what he called "the *accidents* of *individual* Life"

[7] Marginal note in anonymous, *External Punishment Proved to Be Not Suffering, but Privation* (London, 1817), xi. B.M.C. 126, g. 3.

(CL,IV,572). He aspired to transfer to abstraction the attention that poets usually bestow on the physical image. Having survived the collapse of a self-defining physical environment, he made his Life, rather than his individual existence, his subject matter, and his Absolute self became the goal of his meditation. However, even though he strove to see without images, he never entered the mystic's silence, but remained in his own "intermundium," conscious that mere abstractions, like mere images, are false representatives of Being.[8] Christ is man in the fullness of Being, neither a mere man nor a mere metaphor, but a symbol that transcends all accident. In rare moments Coleridge celebrates the joy of a transfigured life, but more often he is the poet of the Christian paradox, enduring the conflict of opposites that cannot be resolved in time. Being is revealed in language by means of paradox, but Being dies in any resolution of paradox, just as the Being of a work of art is distorted by any single interpretation. Paradox can convey the anguish of the human spirit alienated from God yet living in possibility, "death-in-life." And Coleridge wrote: "*I come to cure the Disease, not to explain it*" (AR,283).

In the pages that follow, I have tried to witness Coleridge's struggle to create an authentic poetry of Being. I have emphasized the neglected or, in my view, misunderstood later poems, mainly those following "Dejection: An Ode," which for many ends Coleridge's poetic career. However, I have referred to earlier works whenever they help to clarify some aspects of the poet's struggle with language. And I have made use of the poet's letters, his other prose writings, and particularly his notebooks, in which his most private needs find their "outness." Since Coleridge's art is one that values Being and process more than the unity, coherence, and integrity valued by the "new criticism," I have not provided thorough explications of each late poem. Some poems receive rather extensive commentary, while

---

[8] Coleridge frequently uses "mere" to indicate a crucial limitation, an idea or a thing, divorced from its activating power (see CL,III,481).

others appear only as instances of an ongoing process. As more and more of Coleridge's works appear in the *Collected Coleridge*, I am confident that other writers will explore, in a more comprehensive way, the singular power of his life in poetry—a life that only begins with his "few great poems." Further, as we become more certain of the dates of particular poems, we may be able to read more accurately the poet's progress through time.

The course of development that I have suggested by my sequence of metaphors has, like Coleridge's sacred river, a "mazy motion," but it does approximate the poet's life in art. From a beginning in which some momentary harmony with external nature is discovered ("The Eddy-Rose"), through a period in which he questions the reflective power of nature ("Phantom"), Coleridge enters an imaginary realm ("Limbo") in which he is on the threshold of Being. Finally, in "Beyond Metaphor: Coleridge's Abstract Self" the poet imagines "an unborrow'd self" beyond the conflicting opposites that define our natural existence. This current flowing from the phenomenal to the noumenal is, of course, not consistently steady and progressive, but it does mirror the organic process of human life which, in Coleridge's words, "begins in detachment from Nature, and ends in union with God" (LR,IV,401).

I have tried to make Coleridge's Being "stand forth," as Heidegger says, and also to show that "however irregular and desultory [his] conversation [and poetry] may happen to be, there is Method in the fragments" (TM,9). Treatises on German idealism, opium addiction, plagiarism, and the like, can help us read *into* Coleridge's work, but a study of how he struggled with metaphor and poetic form in order to create a new self can reveal what is already there. I have heeded Coleridge's warning against "the tendency to look abroad, *out* of the thing in question, in order by means of some *other* thing analogous to understand the former. But this is impossible—for the thing in question *is* the act, we are describing" (CN,III,4225). Coleridge's poetic act was an act of Being, and the love of the means was his end. The concluding remark of a very early letter remains true for his entire journey toward his ideal object: "too weary to write a fair copy, or re-arrange my ideas—and I am anxious that you should know me as I am—" (CL,I,398).

"It is, indeed, for the *fragmentary* reader only that I have any scruple."

(AR,236)

"In the child's mind there is nothing fragmentary."

(quoted in Alice D. Snyder, *Coleridge on Logic and Learning*, 127)

# *1. The Eddy-Rose*

IN his verse letter to Sara Hutchinson that was to become "Dejection: An Ode," Coleridge wrote: "to all things I prefer the permanent." Here the poet articulates the sad changes in his personal life—his broken marriage, his diminished imaginative power, his physical suffering—but this letter is more than another lament for the transitory nature of human life, and the "accidents of individual life" (CL,IV,572) that are the materials for poetry. Although the poet feels that the more fixed *idea* of Sara is preferable to her changing presence, he realizes that the conflict between stability and progression, between fixity and disruptive motion, is characteristic of earthly life—of art as well as actual experience. To evade that conflict by retreating into abstractions is a painful error that his Ode dramatizes, and Coleridge ends his poem with a metaphor that reconciles his opposites, yet keeps them clearly distinguishable:

> To her may all things live, from pole to pole,
> Their life the eddying of her living soul!

Coleridge's "eddy" is more than an illustrative metaphor that enlightens a single poem. With such variants as "whirlpool," "whirlwind," and "the circle," it provides a symbolic pattern, revealing the poet's desire to define Being by means of external nature, and anticipating Pound's "Vortex," which Hugh Kenner accurately glosses: "the vortex is not the water but a patterned energy made visible by the water."[1] Coleridge's "eddy" suggests the union of opposing forces, but such a union is not always a happy one, indi-

[1] Hugh Kenner, *The Pound Era* (Berkeley and Los Angeles: University of California Press, 1971), p. 146.

cating as it does movement without progression. Before we can fully appreciate the relation of "eddying" to "life" at the end of the Ode, we must consider other contexts in which the metaphor gains its definitive power.[2]

One of its earlier appearances occurs in a notebook entry of 1797-98. Describing his own children at play, Coleridge vicariously shares in their celebration of life, experiencing the "joy" he will later wish for the absent Sara at the end of his Ode: "the wisdom & graciousness of God in the infancy of the human species . . . the elder whirling for joy, the one in petticoats, a fat Baby, eddying half willingly, half by the force of the Gust—driven backward, struggling forward—both drunk with the pleasure, both shouting their hymn of Joy" (CN,I,330). Coleridge found his children's lack of self-consciousness appealing, and admired their Dionysian delight that is its own artistic expression or "hymn." When the need for a destination is abandoned, inner and outer forces can achieve a balance, a temporary harmony, the means having become the end. Paul Valéry, in his comparison of prose to walking and poetry to dancing, reasons Coleridge's response into a theory. With either poetry or dance, Valéry observes, artistic expression is "not a question of carrying out a limited operation whose end is situated somewhere in our surroundings, but rather of creating, maintaining, and exalting a certain *state*, by a periodic movement that can be executed on the spot."[3]

But in Coleridge's account, significantly, he is an observer, not a participant; and although he longed to take part in a "Bacchanalian whirl," he more often suffered what he called the "dreadful consequences of the interspersed vacancies

[2] John Beer in his recent *Coleridge's Poetic Intelligence* (New York: Harper & Row, 1977) comments on the poet's recurring use of the Eddying figure. Our reading has brought us several of the same examples, but I think our use of the evidence is different.

[3] Paul Valéry, *The Art of Poetry*, trans. Denise Folliot (New York, Pantheon Books, 1958), pp. 70-71.

left in the mind by the absence of Dionysus" (CN,III,3263). These "interspersed vacancies" occur in "Frost at Midnight," and are filled up by a willed act of consciousness that brings human nature into a productive collaboration with the power controlling external nature. Whereas the poet's son Derwent accommodates the wind "*half* willingly," a partial assertion of will could not remain a lasting solution for Coleridge. His ambivalent use of the Eddy metaphor demonstrates the difficulty of keeping mind and world, subject and object, as polar opposites when one desires to achieve Unity of Being. Coleridge's abiding distrust of Pantheism prevented him from finding in the Eddy a true metaphor for Being; for to be sucked into the cycle of nature meant drowning *within* it, rather than rising *through* it. Wordsworth could imagine being carried round in earth's diurnal course, and Keats could resign himself to the eternal process of fruition and decay, but Coleridge never abandoned his belief that human life must be progressive, and that man's will must originate and direct a movement that extends beyond the cycle of the seasons. Man is incomplete but so is Nature, which appears to be complete only because we cannot perceive its origin and its end. Coleridge may occasionally envy the Wordsworthian child, but he also realizes that he cannot reverse evolution and move backward to the "infancy of the human species." Because God exists, Nature itself creates neither form nor matter; hence man is superior to Nature because he may assert his creative will. Separation, not union, is man's means of self-discovery. The unseen power that controls Nature can create its own "magic eddies" (AR,391), but these appear without danger because they suggest a force that precedes time and progression: "Quiet stream, with all its eddies, & the moonlight playing on them, quiet as if they were Ideas in the divine mind anterior to the Creation—" (CN,I,1154). Once the world was created, however, the eddying mind became visible through symbols rather than through forms of matter.

We can find evidence of "life" in nature, but "in our life alone does nature live." Only through acts of consciousness, not through acts of sensory abandonment, can a poet bring natural forms into Being.

As early as 1794 Coleridge had been impressed by the Eddy image in one of Southey's poems that he transcribed. In "On Bala Hill" (PW,I,56-57) Southey associated "eddy" with "life" in a manner that foreshadows the more powerful use of the Eddy image in "Dejection: An Ode." From the heights, the speaker looks down on "The falling leaves of many a faded hue/ That eddy in the wild gust moaning by!/ Ev'n so it far'd with Life! in discontent/ Restless thro' Fortune's mingled scenes I went." Southey's lines parallel Coleridge's early method: to explain life in terms of the phenomenal world, and then by a rationalization to short circuit the power of the imagery by making it serve conventional piety and moral teaching. The poem ends:

> O cease fond heart! in such sad thoughts to roam,
> For surely thou ere long shalt reach thy home,
> And pleasant is the way that lies before.

The concluding line is ironic, for the youthful Coleridge had not yet realized the full import of the metaphor he had discovered. At twenty-two, he was impressed by the relationship of Eddy to Life, but he had not undergone the personal experience that would eventually give the metaphor its full intensity. Whereas conventional sentimental phrases and poetic rhetoric only offered an illusion of unity —they only appeared to reconcile the dynamic opposites of life—Coleridge's Eddy metaphor truly married such opposites. Too strong to be subdued by platitudes, the Eddy retained its life and became the nucleus around which Coleridge's experience, like crystals, began to take on form.

In a notebook entry, over two years before his verse letter to Sara, Coleridge gives a prose account of an experience that I have here arranged into lines and called "The Eddy-Rose":

> River Greta near its
> Fall into the Tees—
> Shootings of water
> Threads down the slope
> Of the huge green stone.
> The white Eddy-rose
> That blossom'd up
> Against the stream in the scollop,
> By fits and starts,
> Obstinate in resurrection—
> It *is the life* that we live.
>
> (CN,I,495; variant, CN,I,1589)

Unlike the casual and easily dismissed image in "On Bala Hill," the Eddy-Rose here evokes a happy epiphany. More than an appreciation of nature's creative power, and beyond the artist's continual struggle with the intractable matter of things and words, it contains a revelation of Being. Of considerable significance is the fact that the rose (and indeed, the poem) is simply a by-product of the dynamic interplay of forces, escaping as it does *out of* an apparently endless circling process. The beauty that blossoms exists in a tension with the natural force of the stream; refusing to be confined by the flow of the material world, it generates itself and persists in blossoming upward. Later, when he rethinks his experience, as he frequently does, Coleridge tries to understand what is behind this phenomenon. When a stream encounters an obstruction or counterforce, an eddy results. But the poet is interested in more than an explanation of cause and effect; he seeks a principle of Being: "hung over the Bridge, & musing considering how much of this Scene of endless variety in Identity was Nature's—how much the living organ's! —What would it be if I had the eyes of a fly!" (CN,I,1589). Coleridge's "poem" provides an answer to this quest for a principle of Being: his consciousness alone makes it possible for him to conceive of form, and he finds that Being is not embodied in natural processes but instead is a spirit ever struggling to shape them. In this blessed moment, Coleridge sees not only things but, like Wordsworth at Tintern Abbey, into the *life* of things. Our awareness of life becomes the life that we live.[4]

Just as the rose has to be continually recreated by the collision of stream and stone, so Coleridge's idea of Being must be endlessly re-established, never simply stated. No insight into life or art can result from an uninterrupted stream of associations, a "stream of consciousness." "Free" association is chaos, and order only becomes recognizable when a controlling intelligence "curbs and rudders" (AP,46) nature's movements. "In every living form," the poet writes, "the conditions of its *existence* are to be sought for in that which is *below* it; the grounds of its *intelligibility* in that which is *above* it."[5] In other words, form includes both the obstruction that causes the eddy, and the mind that "Waltzes on her [nature's] Eddy-Pools" (CL,v,496). This waltzing, self-circling mind performs in what is probably Coleridge's most aesthetically satisfying poem, "Frost at Midnight."

The motion of the film on the grate in "Frost at Midnight" sends the poet into a Proustian evocation of the past, which both defines the present and makes a future order possible. The circular form of the poem, whose end is a meaningful return to its beginning, mirrors the imagination's own motion which "seeks of itself" and is akin to the

---

[4] Robert Frost in "West-Running Brook" makes a similar use of the eddy figure. In a meeting of contraries, the poet discovers a metaphor for human life:

> It is this backward motion toward the source,
> Against the stream, that most we see ourselves in,
> The tribute of the current to the source,
> It is from this in nature we are from.
> It is most us.

*Complete Poems of Robert Frost* (New York: Henry Holt and Co., 1959), p. 329.

[5] *Coleridge: Selected Poetry and Prose*, ed. Stephen Potter (London: Nonesuch Press, 1933), p. 466.

flame because it too is content seeking its form. That the spirit must be "idling" before it can discover itself reflected in nature (by an "echo or mirror") suggests the positive aspect of the Eddy metaphor. One must momentarily resist forward motion in order to realize upward motion; the stream must be curbed before the Eddy-Rose can become visible. The "idling spirit," like the poem itself, serves to define activity and provide the perspective we need in order to see that thought without belief is only a "toy," a diversion from things as they are. The interplay of motion and stasis that characterizes the Eddy metaphor also characterizes "Frost at Midnight." Thus, the final line of the poem, "Quietly shining to the quiet moon," formally resolves Coleridge's dual definition of nature: *natura naturata*, the phenomena as passive ("quiet moon"); and *natura naturans*, the active, vital power that Coleridge knew could never be contained for long in any product ("quietly shining"). By the end of the poem the vacancies, the momentary pauses, and the hush of nature, have been filled. Silent Nature becomes articulate; the "secret ministry" of both frost and poet has been per-formed. The world is neither denied nor given precedence. Rather, it is simply given form, for "language is form."

As Coleridge's writing continues, only at rare moments do we encounter the striking reconciliation of opposites that we find in "The Eddy-Rose" and "Frost at Midnight" —and, of course, "Kubla Khan." Truly, extremes met productively in these instances, but the occasions on which Coleridge's analytic mind, given to "abstruser musings," could be at rest were as rare as holidays. Coleridge could have been referring to such occasions later, when he wrote in *The Friend* of "one of those brief sabbaths of the soul, when the activity and discursiveness of the thoughts are suspended, and the mind quietly *eddies* round, instead of flowing onward—(as at late evening in the Spring I have seen a bat wheel in silent circles round and round a fruit-tree in full blossom") (*Friend*,I,343-44). His principle of beauty

was derived from these demonstrations of peaceful circular-
ity, this "unity in multeity." As he learned from his reading
in Schlegel, "in order to derive pleasure from the occupa-
tion of the mind, the principle of unity must always be
present, so that in the midst of the multeity the centripetal
force be never suspended, nor the sense be fatigued by the
predominance of the centrifugal force" (BL,II,262). It was
not every day that such a balance could be achieved.

Despite the beauty and beauty-making power revealed by
the Eddy-Rose, and the peace resulting from a momentary
surrender to the appearances of nature, Coleridge could not
long be content with a metaphor of Being that did not
contain the idea of progress. His "sabbaths of the soul" were
true holy-days: accompanied by awe, wonder, and sometimes even fear. God was all will, and a child perhaps only
half will, but a man deprived of a self-determined course
was in danger of being sucked into the vortex, as were the
Mariner's lifeless (i.e. will-less) shipmates:

> Upon the whirl, where sank the ship,
> The boat spun round and round.

The same bat that provided an image of the peaceful, idling
soul could also represent the self-hypnotic man who, without method, "flutters about in blindness, like the bat; or
carried hither and thither, like the turtle sleeping on the
wave, and fancying, because he moves, that he is in progress" (TM,5). In his highly imaginative "The Destiny of
Nations," Coleridge conceives of "one all-conscious Spirit"
whose thought is a "self-affirming act"; however the Mo-
nads who execute the divine will have an "end" toward
which they must proceed. With "whirlwind speed," they
perform their tasks, keeping their goal in mind:

> Thus these pursue their never-varying course,
> No eddy in their stream. Others, more wild,
> With complex interests weaving human fates,
> Duteous or proud, alike obedient all,
> Evolve the process of eternal good.
>
> (PW,I,133)

Nature may appear to move in circles, but behind the phenomenal world is an invisible power, providing a direction for everything. Coleridge could accept the circle as a representation of ideal unity, but he could not accept nature if its only purpose was to whirl in an "endless and objectless circle" (PL,223-24).

Coleridge marked the dynamic oppositions that he discovered in his physical world—in waterfalls as well as eddy pools—with the phrase "extremes meet." As a scientific observer he could explain any given phenomenon, but he went beyond a pragmatic explanation and questioned even the *cause* of cause-and-effect. The mystery remained to be confronted, if not explained: "Rest, motion! O ye strange locks of intricate simplicity, who shall find the key? . . . Rest = enjoyment and death. Motion = enjoyment and life. O the depth of the proverb, 'Extremes meet'!"[6] To be a willing participant in God's creation, Coleridge had to ask: extremes meet, but what is the meeting *for?* The poet needed a metaphor that could yoke eddy with progression, stasis with forward motion, in order to be true to his own evolutionary theory. His comments on *King Lear* help us to understand his requirements for both artistic expression and personal existence: Edgar's ravings are productive because they have a "practical end in view," whereas with Lear "there is only the brooding of the one anguish, an eddy without progression" (ShC,I,65). Shakespeare's play as a single unified vision incorporates both characters; it is like "the hurricane and the whirlpool, absorbing as it advances" (ShC,I,54). Whether the Eddy be external or internal, its engaging forces must find an outlet. The maddening effect of an "eddying" mind is described in "The Two Founts":

> Who then needs wonder, if (no outlet found
> In passion, spleen, or strife) the Fount of Pain
> O'erflowing beats against its lovely mound,
> And in wild flashes shoots from heart to brain?
>
> (PW,I,455)

[6] Potter, *Coleridge: Selected Poetry and Prose*, p. 180.

23

Coleridge's own dejection, as we know, occurred when he could find "no natural outlet."

The forward-moving stream is finally the controlling metaphor for Coleridge, whether it momentarily achieves the sublime marriage of motion and rest in a waterfall, or acquires the hypnotic power of an eddy. A very early notebook entry establishes an analogy that underlies the poet's struggle to distinguish eddying and progressive motion: "truth is compared in scripture to a streaming fountain; if her waters flow not in perpetual progression, they stagnate into a muddy pool of conformity & tradition" (CN,I,119). An eddy, like the bat that wheels in silent circles round and round a fruit tree, is certainly more cause for delight and wonder than a stagnant pool, but it still serves poorly as an image of life because it leads nowhere. All of Coleridge's "Principles of Method" aim at producing a linear sequence; he described history as a "living line," and felt that philosophy "should be bonâ fide progressive, not in circulo—productive not barren" (CL,IV,917). Coleridge believed that poetry, on the other hand, demanded another principle: the Neoplatonic circle that completes itself. In both cases his allegiance was to progressive movement. Looking back in his later years, he considered his "too great continuity of mind" to be the reason he had failed to complete so many poems and projects. "In short," he wrote, "in every thing *Continuity* is the characteristic both Quality and Property of my Being" (CL,VI,729). An Eddy-Rose or a Kubla Khan appear as natural anomalies, to be wondered at before moving on. Rather than completed objects of art, they are fragments of an ongoing life, skins that the snake leaves behind.

Coleridge felt that Wordsworth's life and art were unified, and that the poet was capable of resolutely avoiding both the stagnant pool and the whirlpool, unlike the preachers Coleridge heard in his final year, who "never progress; they eddy round and round. Sterility of mind follows their ministry" (TT, Jan. 7, 1833). Although he had identified

Wordsworth's weakness as "occasional prolixity, repetition, and an eddying, instead of progression, of thought" (BL,II,-109), Coleridge knew, after listening to his idol read from *The Prelude*, that Wordsworth had never been driven off course by either external or internal forces. His acts were "currents self-determined" and, regardless of circumstances, his power "streamed" from him. The poem "To William Wordsworth" (PW,I,403-08) ends with a clear declaration of the power of our human will to avoid being "drowned" in the "turbulent," and to discover instead those "chosen Laws controlling choice,/ Action and joy!—An Orphic song indeed,/ A song divine of high and passionate thoughts/ To their own music chaunted!" Coleridge was well aware that his own diseased will had chosen badly, and that he had fallen victim to the whirlpool Charybdis. His despair was "not to be cured by opposites, which for the most part only reverse the symptoms while they exasperate the Disease—or like a Rock in the Mid Channel of a River swoln by a sudden rain-flush from the mountain, which only detains the excess of Waters from their proper Outlet, and makes them foam, roar, and eddy" (AR,86).

When Coleridge later wrote his own "Orphic song," he was able to draw two portraits, one of his admired friend and one of himself. Wordsworth, as "Nature's Confessor," knows what he *should* know, and achieves stability by moving ever forward, not looking back at Eurydice; whereas Coleridge, "plucking the poisons of self-harm," chooses to probe the forbidden:

### Orpheus

Tho' with the Vulgar
Strange Customs lead to blind Conjectures, what
The curious Wench discusses with the Laundress
And then takes council of the key-hole, that
The Man, whose Science Practice still impregnates,
Sees at one glance. *He's Nature's Confessor!*
To *him* she opens out her tale of Wrongs,

And in the sequels (Eye, Look, Gestures, Moods)
Engraves the history of the causing Acts.
Lock'd doors & curtain'd Windows prove vain
   safe-guards.
The sole sure plan the Theban Women taught,
Who tore wise Orpheus piece-meal. Tho' no Tell-tale,
He had pierc'd backwards into Deeds unseen:
And woe to Him, who being guiltless knows,
Or is thought to know, a lurking Guilt! For Shame,
That leads not to Amendment, wakes Revenge.
(CN,III,4286)

The duality of the Orphean myth, which embodies both the
creative power of song and the destructive power of transgression, seems to epitomize the two poets' lives. God-like,
Wordsworth seems to move among the forms of nature,
inferring and conferring life, his song synthesizing man and
nature, the poet and his poem. In Wordsworth's world,
God is never provoked to acts of revenge because His
taboos are respected, and Nature itself reveals to the poet
the Being hidden behind appearances. It was Coleridge who
followed the "Orphic song" to its end, suffering punishment
at the hands of the Maenads. His secret sin, of which opium
addiction was but a manifestation, lured him toward de-
struction, and he wrote that vices "urge me on, just like
the feeling of an Eddy-Torrent to a swimmer" (CN,III,-
4166). Coleridge's quarrel with Wordsworth revealed that
Wordsworth was unable to comprehend Coleridge's weaknesses. As he wrote in old age, an eddy was, for Wordsworth, but an "emblem" for the moral instruction of a
"stranger":

> Behold an emblem of our human mind
> Crowded with thoughts that need a settled home,
> Yet, like to eddying balls of foam
> Within this whirlpool, they each other chase
> Round and round, and neither find
> An outlet nor a resting-place!

Stranger, if such disquietude be thine,
Fall on thy knees and sue for help divine.[7]

Wordsworth made his journey into "the deep recesses
of man's heart" and returned healthy, calm, and secure. His
"self-determination" was possible because he enjoyed a
monistic sense of selfhood. But Coleridge, as "Orpheus" reveals, was ever divided, being both Orpheus and Eurydice.
That his fears were "fears self-willed" did not make them
any less real. The poet lamented "the effect of *selfness* in a
mind incapable of gross Self-interest—decrease of Hope and
Joy, the Soul in its round & round flight forming narrower
circles, till at every Gyre its wings beat against the *personal
Self*" (CN,II,2531). To be caught in an eddy of self-defini-
tion was to be little better than a brute animal "driven
round in the unvarying circles of Instinct" (*Friend*,I,190n),
or a sensualist caught in "the wide gust-eddying stream of
our desires and aversions" (*Friend*,I,444). As the opium
habit ate at Coleridge's freedom of will, he was compelled
to acknowledge his vulnerability before a power greater
than the power of opium. Suffering spiritual vertigo, he
could not right himself on a direct course, and instead,
visualized himself accelerating toward some "great sea-
vortex."

The eventual conclusion of this dizzying, self-circling
movement was, as Coleridge knew, madness. He wrote that
"a rooted hatred, an inveterate thirst of revenge, is a sort of
madness, and still eddies round its favourite object, and exercises as it were a perpetual tautology of mind. . . . Like a
fish in a globe of glass, it moves restlessly round and round
the scanty circumference, which it cannot leave without
losing its vital element" (PW,II,1099). The poet had
watched his young son Hartley whirling and eddying like
a blossom in a breeze, but he also witnessed, as the boy grew

[7] "Inscription on the Banks of a Rocky Stream," *The Poetical
Works of William Wordsworth*, ed. E. de Selincourt and Helen
Darbishire (Oxford: Clarendon Press, 1947), IV, 208.

into manhood, his decline into dissipation and purposelessness. Coleridge could accurately diagnose Hartley's disease because he had experienced it himself: a debilitating, defective will. But unlike his father, Hartley "had an absence of any contra-distinguishing Self, any conscious 'I' " (CL,v,-110). Coleridge was fearfully aware of the "end" he was approaching, and it seemed little different from the one he had predicted for brute animals and sensualists: "what more natural than that the mental striving should become an eddy?—madness may perhaps be defined as the circling in a stream which should be progressive and adaptive" (MC,102). King Lear's loss of sanity brought, at least, a simultaneous release from the strictures of logic ("O matter and impertinency mixed. Reason in madness"). But possessing as he did a clear conception of his own duality, Coleridge imagined for himself a state far more terrible: he called it "conscious madness."

Regardless of the danger, Coleridge felt compelled to confront the destructive aspect of his Eddy metaphor in order to approach Ultimate Being. Perhaps the poet had to enter the eddy before he could outgrow his personal self and generate a new "absolute self." In his later years, he pointed out to his son, Derwent, the danger he had survived: "For O! my dear dear Boy! never forget, that as there is a Self-willedness which drifts away from self-interest to finish it's course in the sucking eddy-pool of Selfishness, so there is a Self-interest which begins in Self-sacrifice, and ends in God" (CL,v,82). Coleridge had, perhaps, drifted into that eddy-pool of selfishness, but he was able to will his own resurrection, like the Eddy-Rose:

> The white Eddy-rose
> That blossom'd up
> Against the stream in the scollop,
> By fits and starts,
> Obstinate in resurrection—
> It *is the life* that we live.

28

The words of both poem and letter recall the Christian incarnation that transfigures ordinary experience. Another visionary, William Blake, could have welcomed Coleridge as a "traveller through eternity" who sees:

> That every thing has its
> Own Vortex; and when once a traveller thro' Eternity
> Has passd that Vortex, he perceives it roll backward behind
> His path, into a globe itself infolding; like a sun:
> Or like a moon, or like a universe of starry majesty,
> While he keeps onwards in his wondrous journey on the earth.[8]

The disturbance or counterforce that causes a current to run against its ordinary course was, as we have seen, both a creative and a destructive force for Coleridge; negative Being (doubt) was, perhaps, a necessary condition of his Belief. To achieve a balance of opposing forces, without eliminating their "life" or power, was perhaps the need underlying Coleridge's writing in general, not just his poetry. The Eddy becomes a whirlwind in one late letter:

> In all subjects of deep and lasting Interest you will detect a struggle between two opposites, two polar Forces, both of which are alike necessary to our human Well-being, & necessary each to the continued existence of the other—Well therefore may we contemplate with intense feelings those whirlwinds which are, for free-agents, the appointed means & only possible condition of that *equi-librium*, in which our moral Being subsists: while the disturbance of the same constitutes our sense of Life. (CL,v,35)

Like the earlier Eddy-Rose, this whirlwind is more than an analogue for the circular Romantic poem. Again we encounter a meeting of opposites that generates a synthesis:

---

[8] *Milton: Book The First, The Poetry and Prose of William Blake*, ed. David V. Erdman (New York: Doubleday Anchor, 1965), p. 108.

29

our Being remains fixed while we *feel* our Life changing, flowing onward. Here there is no mystical yearning for transcendence, for Coleridge rejects mystics when they attempt an arbitrary break with the world. He would agree with Teilhard de Chardin that the mystics failed to see that their "mystical night or death could only be the end and apotheosis of a process of growth."[9] Coleridge's whirlwind achieves the paradoxical union of movement and stasis that we find in the famous moon gloss to "The Ancient Mariner," where the stars "still sojourn, yet still move onward." Through an act of contemplation, or by means of a poem, we can temporarily arrest movement and apprehend our Being, but we must never forget that there is a guiding force impelling the flow and that we are temporary sojourners committed to a further journey. "Our mortal existence," Coleridge said, "what is it but a stoppage in the flood of life, a brief eddy from wind or concourse of currents in the overflowing ocean of pure activity?" (AP,184)

The progressive circle becomes the metaphor that satisfies Coleridge's hunger for ideal permanence within a mutable world. But in order to conceive of that composite image, the poet needed to separate himself from external nature, and make himself his own object of contemplation. Both poem and physical phenomenon must be seen as only momentary demonstrations of a continuing power, and self-reflection is necessary before both can be kept in subordinate positions: "the whole process is cyclical tho' progressive, and the Man separates from Nature only that Nature may be found again in a higher dignity in the Man" (CL,IV,769). The centrifugal and centripetal forces of Coleridge's life appear to have achieved their "equi-librium" in his later years, but the balance had to be earned and, like Lear, the poet had to enter the whirlwind in order to gain knowledge. In this context, the often-noted definition of "Symbol" in *The Statesman's Manual* takes on a fuller mean-

[9] Pierre Teilhard de Chardin, *The Future of Man* (London: Collins, 1964), p. 56.

ing and becomes more than a simple literary definition: the poet celebrates "that reconciling and mediatory power, which incorporating the Reason in Images of the Sense, and organizing (as it were) the flux of the Senses by the permanence and self-circling energies of the Reason, gives birth to a system of symbols, harmonious in themselves, and consubstantial with the truths, of which they are the *conductors*. These are the Wheels which Ezekiel beheld" (LS,29). Like Blake, Coleridge knew that "what is Above is Within," and that "the Circumference still expands going forward to Eternity."[10] Moreover, for both poets Ezekiel's wheels oppose the "cogs tyrannic" of mechanistic or materialistic philosophy.

With our awareness of Coleridge's various uses of the Eddy metaphor, we can return to "Dejection: An Ode," in an attempt to add significance to the relationship between Eddying and Life in the final stanza. Offering his benediction to the absent Sara, Coleridge ends his poem:

> With light heart may she rise,
> Gay fancy, cheerful eyes,
> Joy lift her spirit, joy attune her voice;
> To her may all things live, from pole to pole,
> Their life the eddying of her living soul!
> O simple spirit, guided from above,
> Dear Lady! friend devoutest of my choice,
> Thus mayest thou ever, evermore rejoice.

The things of nature are merely "lifeless shapes" unless Sara's own Being can inspirit them, and here again Coleridge demonstrates his distinction between *natura naturata* and *natura naturans*, nature made and nature making. But in this instance, as in the final lines of "Frost at Midnight," Coleridge anticipates their possible collaboration. Because nature is "that which is *about to be born*, that which is always *becoming*" (AR,244), the Eddying might suggest

---

[10] Erdman, *Milton: Book The First*, p. 223.

spiritual energy trapped in physical nature, caught in a meaningless repetition, yet struggling to be free. On the other hand, the poet (and Sara is but a projection or surrogate of himself) possesses both the energy and will to channel the self-circling pattern into a productive direction. Reality or "Ultimate Being," as Coleridge once defined it, is "the union of the actual and the potential." Man and nature are united in a dance of possibility. The word "may" appears six times in the final stanza: *may* all things live, *mayst* thou rejoice.

The duality of the Eddy metaphor functions in "Dejection: An Ode," for its creative or regenerative aspect and its negative and destructive one both operate there. Progressive movement is again stated in terms of flowing water: the poet's fountain source, his "soul," does not "issue forth." He has life without life's "effluence." The movement from inner to outer nature has been impeded, but even while he lacks confidence in himself the poet possesses confidence in the principle by which diverse material manifestations are subordinated to their source of Being: that single inner source from which "flows all that charms or ear or sight,/ All melodies the echoes of that voice,/ All colours a suffusion from that light." Progressive movement has been retarded not only by "abstruse research" but, paradoxically, by self-circling thinking itself. The poet seems as rudderless as he appears in a notebook entry when he imagines himself "Whirled about without a center—as in a nightmair—no gravity—a vortex without a center" (CN,III,3999).

The distraught penultimate stanza, preceding the restorative balance suggested by the Eddy metaphor in the final stanza, should probably be considered an essential part of the complete symbolic complex. Coleridge, as we have seen, feared the self-circling mind headed for madness as much as he desired the self-circling mind that evolves form. Here the poet's morbid imagination creates sick images of vipers that "coil around" his mind. Like a swimmer sucked into a whirlpool, the poet is only an involuntary spectator to the random workings of nature, a passive victim of his own deranged imaginings. Inner and outer worlds are hopelessly confused, and "reality" has become a "dark dream." The scream of agony released by the Aeolian harp represents the poet's fear of being driven mad in a world he cannot control. He can project the positive, creative aspect of the Eddy onto Sara, but he must retain, even cherish, the negative aspect himself—or else be drawn into non-Being. He wrote: "O God! when a man blesses the loud Scream of Agony that awakens him, night after night. . ." (CL,II,990). Even a sick shaping spirit of imagination is more companionable than the dark dream in which both pleasure and pain are illusory. The wind "rav'st" and is a "Mad Lutanist." The haphazard images that form this stanza suggest a mind that has been severed from its mooring, one that has lost all sequential order. The speaker's "frenzy" is the result of his inability to find order in the chaos that he himself has created.

After this mad eddying, the storm subsides and the other, more healthy face of the image appears. Unlike the "mad dream" of reality, in which thoughts dominate the thinker, now his discursive mind moves Coleridge away from the destructive capacities of the Eddy and toward its beneficial aspect, although in both verse epistle and Ode the ending is tentative. One *should* or *may* enjoy experience:

> Thus, thus shoulds't thou rejoice!
> To thee would all things live from pole to pole,
> Their Life the Eddying of thy living Soul.
> (CL,II,798)

> To her may all things live, from pole to pole,
> Their life the eddying of her living soul!
> ("Dejection: An Ode")

As in other Coleridge poems, the "conclusion" occurs not within experience but beyond it, and is characteristically projected onto another person, another "self" to represent

his "ulterior consciousness." As the Eddy-Rose demonstrates, life is continually forming itself—Coleridge looked
with favor on the Greek line "God always forming himself"
(CN,III,4237)—and rising above its natural elements. Likewise, in his Ode the poet creates a new self that transcends
the limitations of his own personal history. Since he believed
in these two separate levels of reality, Coleridge was reluctant to conclude either his poems or his life on the lower
level.

In "The Night-Scene," a fragment of an historical
drama, Coleridge creates a parallel to the central problem
of his Ode: the conflict between limitless life and confining
form. Again, living is seen as a flowing stream, and eyes
are "suffused" with rapture. Joy or blessedness, rising
above mere pleasure, produces a marriage of body and
soul, man and nature, internal and external power:

> Life was in us:
> We were all life, each atom of our frames
> A living soul—
>
> (PW,I,422)

Opposites are balanced in an "intense repose" that is not a
passive dream state but a dynamic act of Being. Rejecting
the oriental god "who floats on a Lotos leaf," Coleridge
portrays instead a god who reconciles opposites and speaks
out of the whirlwind:

> The whirl-blast comes, the desert-sands rise up
> And shape themselves; from Earth to Heaven they
> stand,
> As though they were the pillars of a temple,
> Built by Omnipotence in its own honour!
> But the blast pauses, and their shaping spirit
> Is fled: the mighty columns were but sand,
> And lazy snakes trail o'er the level ruins!

The Whirl-blast, like the Eddy, generates a form that rises
out of a dynamic process, but nature proves to be a dead

thing without a "shaping spirit" acting in or upon it. External nature, like the poet's alphabet, is a collection of materials that may appear to shape themselves, as images appeared to shape themselves into "Kubla Khan." However, since nature's *origin* is supernatural, nature itself can create nothing; only the poet's "as though" can make a temple with mighty columns where just sand and ruins exist. Again, only through acts of human consciousness can natural forms declare Being. "Where there is no discontinuity there can be no origination," Coleridge asserts in *Aids to Reflection*, "and every appearance of origination in Nature is but a shadow of our own casting" (AR,258). The "eddying" of Sara's "living" soul bestows "life" on external things, just as the poet's Orphic song resurrects a lifeless language. The participles "eddying" and "living"—like "shining" at the end of "Frost at Midnight"—give vital meaning to the abstraction that we call "life." The famous line should perhaps be read not as an harmonious equation:

Their life [is] the eddying of her living soul

but as a profoundly subordinating relationship:

Their life [but] the eddying of her living soul.

Both "life" and "joy" represent experience that Coleridge is trying to incorporate in the final stanza of his Ode. Both evoke states of Being in which changing particulars are absorbed into a oneness that resembles "A Lake—or if a stream, yet flowing so softly, so unwrinkled, that its flow is *Life* not Change—/ —That state, in which all the individuous nature, the distinction without Division, of a vivid Thought is united with the sense and substance of intensest Reality—" (CN,III,3705). For Coleridge, joy was not simply pleasure, an activity of the body associated with hedonism; but neither was it simply happiness, an unwilled condition resulting from the chance flowering of circumstances. Joy was a blessedness of Being, the soul's eddying in the stream of life. "For what you *are*, you cannot have," he wrote in another fragment of verse suggested by Sara (CN,III,4119), recalling "and man became a living soul." The poet commented on the Biblical statement: "he did not merely *possess* it, he *became* it. It was his proper *being*, his truest *self*, *the* man *in* the man."[11] In his benediction at the end of "Dejection: An Ode," Coleridge creates a composite metaphor in the phrase "the eddying of her living soul," uniting his definition of an evolving and progressive, *natural* life with his definition of a circular poetic *form*, "the snake with it's Tail in it's Mouth" (CL,IV,545). He recorded a similar juxtaposition once when he saw a cataract: "the continual *change* of the *Matter*, the perpetual *Sameness* of the *Form*—it is an awful Image and Shadow of God & the World" (CL,II,853-54). Sara will continue to move through changing time, but her Being, like the poet's own, is permanent.

Whether imagining a creative or destructive Eddy, a self-confining or self-liberating circle, Coleridge demanded that his idea of Being not exclude life's disruptive motion in order to produce an aesthetic object. When the stream of life meets the counterforce of an artist's will a fragment of experience may result, but not all artists are able to forge fragments into coherent works of art. Coleridge recognized that *Paradise Lost*, in combining Christian history and poetic myth, achieved ultimate form: "it and it alone really possesses a beginning, a middle, and an end; it has the totality of the poem as distinguished from the *ab ova* and parentage, or straight line, of history" (LR,I,172). Yet when he wrote his own poems he rarely emulated this self-sufficient form: his theory of organicism impelled his lines forward but often provided no satisfactory means of containing the flow. Thus he could write about "the heat, bustle, and overflowing of a mind, too vehemently pushed on from within to be regardful of the object, upon which it

[11] Quoted in Stephen Potter, *Coleridge and S.T.C.* (London: Jonathan Cape, 1935), pp. 193-94.

was moving" (CL,II,959). By rejecting "pre-conceived" form, accepting the priority of Being over art, Coleridge needed to generate a new idea of form that could liberate him from the dead letter of the poetic law. The poet's use of the Eddy metaphor reveals how difficult it was for him to find any simple shape for the complexities of his personal experience. His obsessive fear of Pantheism, of being swamped by the material world, kept him from finding lasting satisfaction in any celebration of external nature; and his fear of God kept him from being long satisfied with the self-circling Romantic poem whose "inward, downward" spiraling he felt would take him into the "eddy-pool of selfishness." Coleridge believed that one must move through the eddy or whirlwind, as one moves through the body, because "all form as body, i.e. as shape, & not as forma efformans, is dead" (CN,III,4066). He never denied the mind's coherence, but a poem, a by-product of the process of living, was for him but a momentary revelation of Being, fragmentary and inconclusive, because any resolution in this world partakes of death.

"In vain would we derive it [the idea of Being] from the organs of sense; for these supply only surfaces, undulation, phantoms!"

(*Friend*,1,514)

# 2. *Phantom*

WITH the Eddy metaphor, Coleridge was able to express the dynamic interplay of opposites that could, in rare moments, achieve an equilibrium in the physical world, an apprehension of Being. But no metaphor could be conclusive, and as the poet progressed in time he continued to seek "the true and abiding *reality*" (AR,87) beyond the world's appearances. Coleridge's spelling of "phaenomena" emphasizes its root meaning of "appearing,"[1] and just as things observed are not things in themselves, so a metaphor drawn from the sensory world is ever in danger of becoming only an appearance, a ghost, or a "Phantom." The poet's uncertainty about the power of poetry to express Being is revealed in his use of "Phantom," which like the Eddy metaphor, reveals both negative and positive aspects. A Phantom can be a nightmare figure producing fear and dread, but it can also be a beneficent agent of ultimate Being, as in "Apologia Pro Vita Sua":

> The poet in his lone yet genial hour
> Gives to his eyes a magnifying power:
> Or rather he emancipates his eyes
> From the black shapeless accidents of size—
> In unctuous cones of kindling coal,
> Or smoke upwreathing from the pipe's trim bole,
> His gifted ken can see
> Phantoms of sublimity.
>
> (PW,I,345;CN,II,2402)

[1] Coleridge wanted more, he said, than "the evidence that can be derived from *Phaenomena* (= *appearing* things from the Greek verb)" (CL,IV,789).

The Phantom becomes another metaphor for Coleridge's struggle with metaphor.

The title "Phantom" that Ernest Hartley Coleridge assigned to the eight "lines" he found in Coleridge's notebook, (PW,I,393;CN,III,3291), could be misleading to a reader unfamiliar with the poet's particular uses of Phantom in his other writings. The title could determine, hence limit, our responses to the lines that follow. Rather than illustrating its title, the poem seeks its meaning in the life we find outside of dictionaries. Rejecting both the subjective idealist who would divorce the world from its physical moorings and transform it into a shadow or phantom, and the materialist who would banish man's spirit entirely, Coleridge attempted with his Phantom metaphor to explore his ambiguous personal relationships with both external nature and language. Certainly his "lines" are not meant to suggest the existence of a counterfeit appearance, an apparition; nor do they deny the importance of our physical being, for the poet knew that "we cannot arrive at the knowledge of the living Being but thro' the Body which is its Symbol" (CN,III,4066). In "Phantom," the Orphean poet liberates Being from its physical stage, leaving behind a dead body of confining form. But in other poems, as we shall see, Coleridge allows his metaphor to change its meaning as his own feelings change and as he amplifies his idea of Being. Resisting conclusive definition, Coleridge's poetry demonstrates his perpetual act of defining.

### Phantom

All look and likeness caught from earth,
All accident of kin and birth,
Had pass'd away. There was no trace
Of aught on that illumined face,
Uprais'd beneath the rifted stone
But of one spirit all her own;—
She, she herself, and only she,
Shone through her body visibly.

(PW,I,393)

The poem "Phantom" is perhaps Coleridge's purest apprehension of unified Being. Dissolving the intellectual categories by which we claim to define (and master) experience, the poet would further free human vision from any dependence on eyesight, allowing us to *"see by the eyes/ yet know*[,] *feel nothing of the eyes* while we/ *are seeing"* (CN,III,3520n). The distinction between idea and image, for example, seems unsatisfying when discussing an evocation of Being that undermines the ultimate value of language categories. The woman and her image (in one version the sixth line reads: "But of one image all her own"), her spirit and her body, are united by Coleridge in what is both a figuring and a transfiguring act. The visible shining of Being, like the icicles in "Frost at Midnight" that are "quietly shining to the quiet Moon," is not a delusive apparition. Death is the only Phantom in this poem, for the poet could never believe that "Death could come from the living Fountain of Life; Nothingness and Phantom from the Plenitude of Reality! the Absoluteness of Creative Will!" (AR,393).

Coleridge tried to apprehend the "Plenitude of Reality" by means of his poetic imagination, for even when he employed philosophical terms such as "time" and "space" he understood that the philosopher's clear conceptions could never convey the *feeling* of Being that must in time remain unfixed. Poetry, however, as an outgrowth of feeling, could become his means of finding a form to unite Being and the physical life that engenders it. Because the human body or the body of a poem is only a "visible sign of Being," the poet labors to purge language of its phaenomenal dross, and as he "melts & bedims the Image, still leaves in the Soul its living meaning—" (CN,III,4066). To offer a poetic image as a portrait of Being is as absurd as giving God a "place" in heaven. Coleridge questions: "is not rather Place the phantom, which our limited faculties create, as the *picture*, the *word*, of our own *State* of Being" (CN,III,4341). In the imagination's dream, Coleridge was able to "bedim the

Image" of Sara Hutchinson so as to enjoy her "living Spirit." His feeling "created its appropriate form" (CN,II, 2055).

But a poet must deal with images, even while denying their efficacy, just as love must have an object before it can find itself. Coleridge's frustrated love for Sara Hutchinson brought about a need to overpower the Phantom materiality of words and make them serve his spiritual ends. Even when face to face with his love object, he found himself "seeming to look thro' her and asking for her very Self within or even beyond her apparent Form (CN,III,3370).² Clearly Coleridge is not choosing *between* the physical woman and his ideal conception of her; neither does his poem, as his editor states, "illustrate" an idea, suggesting the supremacy of idea over image and the disparity between the two. What Coleridge sought was a metaphor of Being and not a traditional metaphor, for he believed that "all metaphors are grounded on an *apparent* likeness of things essentially different" (AR,138). Only by transforming his metaphors into "symbols" could the poet mediate between physical and spiritual states. In "Phantom," Coleridge shows that metaphor and analogy ("all look and likeness") are not essential to Being, which discovers its own life only after discarding worldly "accidents." The apparition-like woman in the poem may be literally dead or simply beyond the world's determining power, but she seems to have apprehended her Being only after outgrowing her dependence on time and space. Her transfiguration has been achieved—the past tense is significant here—but the poet in his present state of consciousness shares in the "intense repose" he has created from his own inner conflicts: "herself & the Conscience of that self, beyond the bounds of that form which her eyes behold when she looks up on herself/ O there is a form which seems irrelative to imprisonment of Space!" (CN,II,3146).

Even though Coleridge sometimes achieved these mo-

---

² Coleridge emphasized that one's feeling for a person is separable from one's image of that person (CN,II,2061,2078).

ments of sublimity, when his Being was released from its confining form, he never ignored the conflicts out of which such moments arose. He remained alert to the danger that the poem itself could become a "Phaenomenon," a phantom *ens reale* and not a medium to be seen through. The crucial change in a line of the poem "Phantom," from "Shown in her body visibly" (1805) to "Shown thro' her body visibly" (1808), indicates Coleridge's persistent desire to escape from the *merely* apparent. Annotating his own *Statesman's Manual* late in his life, he refers to "the life and light of nature which shines in it [just as God] fills, and shines through, nature." Coleridge never used the words "in" and "through" as casual prepositions, indifferently interchangeable. They indicate not only his struggle to define man's relationship to "nature," but also his problem with the foundations of poetic art: the image as a representation, and the external world as the only object of sense perception. He never denied the particular, but he never stopped questioning its ultimate value. Thus, before quoting "Phantom" in his notebook, he discusses "Love in Sleep," concluding that "a certain indistinctness, a sort of *universal-in-particularness* of Form, seems necessary" before Being can be discovered (CN,II,2441). Like Blake before him, he chose the word "translucent," rather than transparent, to describe that medium, whether it be earth or language, that is imperfect yet can let light pass through while diffusing it. The physical thing can be penetrated by the light of consciousness until it surrenders what the poet called variously "its very self," "its sole self," "its own self."

Despite Coleridge's need to diminish the primacy of the physical image, he could never be contemptuous of the physical world on which he grounded his idea of organic form. Here we must distinguish ideal purity from the process of achieving it. In his deliberately fragmentary poem "Reason" (PW,I,487), Coleridge speculates on ideal Being, but he admits that he can never know the transparency of Dante's "Heart of Light" or the *lumens seccio* of Newton:

43

Whene'er the mist, that stands 'twixt God and thee,
Defecates to a pure transparency,
That intercepts no light and adds no stain—
There Reason is, and there begins her reign!

The poem immediately breaks off with a resigned "But alas!" and ends with a fragment from Dante that blames its blocked transcendence upon "falso immaginar." However, the impossibility of achieving mystical union was never doubted by Coleridge, who shunned "the relaxing Malaria of the Mystic Divinity, which affects to languish after an extinction of individual Consciousness" (CL,VI,555). It is a fully awake consciousness that focuses on the woman whose Being is the "substance" of "Phantom." She *herself* shines through her body, but it is the corresponding consciousness of the observer that transforms sense perception ("visibly") into a form for Being. Coleridge has turned a particular Sara into a "symbol" that, in the poet's well-known definition, "is characterized by a translucence of the Special in the Individual, or of the General in the Especial, or of the Universal in the General." Her inner Being has evolved "through" her outer form, with "through" suggesting both *in spite of* and *by means of*.

The manner in which Coleridge "concludes" his fragment "Reason" with a quotation from Dante perhaps indicates that he knew he was moving toward an imageless vision. As his letters show, Coleridge was reading *The Divine Comedy* with care in his later years and he probably realized that he was faced with a problem similar to Dante's: that of representing ultimate Being in poetry. Dante's pilgrim leaves behind in Purgatory his physical sight (what Coleridge would call his "understanding") and approaches the object of vision. Coleridge's own poetic development more closely resembles that of the pilgrim than that of the Catholic poet creating him; for Dante claimed to have achieved an ultimate vision of God, and aspired, through defective memory and words, to recover what had been lost. There is a preordained, intellectual order to Dante's poem, and his pilgrim passes through preconceived stages. Coleridge's use of light in "Phantom" differs significantly from Dante's use of it in the *Paradiso*. The spirit's light, or ultimate Being, shines *through* (or in the early version "in") the body, but it is never identified as part of the physical object. To entertain fixed concepts of heaven and hell would nullify Coleridge's theory of organic form, of becoming nature. Desiring to pass beyond nature, he could still accept only a perfecting, not a perfected, vision. The highest vision in Dante is unmediated, indeed unapproachable, by the imagination and its images; the highest vision Coleridge can imagine is a "spirit" that maintains some communion, no matter how tenuous, with its phenomenal body. Coleridge denies himself Dante's *visio intellectualis*.

The poem "Phantom" reveals a poet striving to create a naked language for Being, a speech for the "abstract self" that would still be poetry. Coleridge longed for "a more perfect language than that of words—the language of God himself, as uttered by nature" (TL,17). But he remained a poet at battle with the intractable *matter* of language, particularly with his own metaphors, which he distrusted because of their tendency to convey mere phantom appearances rather than actual life and Being. The meaning of metaphor presumes a kinship with a world Coleridge hoped to outgrow. "The purpose of a Metaphor," he wrote, "is to illustrate a something less known by a partial identification of it with some other thing better understood, or at least more familiar" (AR,312). Within the realm of the picturable, true Being could assume only Phantom disguises; consequently, the "more familiar" aspects of Sara Hutchinson, "All accident of kin and birth," had to be left behind in her movement toward unified Being, just as the poet in "Apologia Pro Vita Sua" had to *emancipate* his vision "from the black shapeless accidents of size."[3] The poet could not de-

[3] Coleridge makes a remark that could be salutary to contemporary

pend on the objective world to provide images for his thought or his feeling, which he described as "an act of consciousness having itself for its only Object" (CN,III, 3605). Worldly analogy tends to link an artist with worldly ends, thus Coleridge needed to weaken the vehicle of traditional metaphor in order to empower its tenor. The demands Coleridge placed on himself and poetry were almost superhuman: he wanted to present not a face but "the apotheosis of the Face" (CN,III,3405), and further, to release Being from the "rifted stone" of traditional poetic language.

A moving notebook entry written in 1808 demonstrates Coleridge's acute awareness of the difficulty of creating a language appropriate to his evolving recognition of Being. Observing a most ordinary event—a bird dropping excrement—the poet refuses to be confined by the literal fact itself and, like Hopkins later, attempts to penetrate the inner Being of this commonplace thing: "the soil that fell from the Hawk poised at the extreme boundary of Sight thro' a column of sunshine—a falling star, a gem, the fixation, & chrystal, of substantial Light, again dissolving & elongating like a liquid Drop—how altogether lovely this to the Eye, and to the Mind too while it remained its own self, all & only its very Self" (CN,III,3401). As in the poem "Phantom," inner Being is revealed by a "substantial" light, and the observer desires to share in the act of a subject discovering "its own self" within nature and to resist the urge to shape the experience into a poetic object. After declaring the futility of simply naming and identifying the event ("What a wretched Frenchman would not he be, who could shout out—charming Hawk's *Turd!*"), Coleridge proceeds from his delightful observation to a consideration of love

---

"confessional" poets: "it is for the Biographer, not the Poet, to give the *accidents* of *individual* Life. What ever is not representative, generic, may be indeed most poetically exprest, but is not Poetry" (CL,IV,572).

and Being. Once more he wishes that language would reach beyond "associations accidental," just as he wanted Sara's self in "Phantom" to be "She, she herself, and only she," without metaphoric debasement. Seeing must be "more than an act of mere sight," and true vision cannot be described because words "involve association of other words as well as other thoughts": thus, what begins in powerful and pure feeling ends in "vulgar association." Coleridge aspired to use poetry as a means of revealing Being, not to use Being merely as material for his poems. At the end of his notebook entry, he openly envies the Polyclete who, beyond Phantom metaphors, "thought in acts, not words— energy divinely languageless" (CN,III,3401).

But Coleridge was too garrulous to be a God acting in silence, and he never ceased using poetry in his attempt to get beyond poetry. Although he often resisted the restrictions of "confining form" in life or language, he realized that words could at least help reveal Being. To believe that the "powerful feelings" that Wordsworth expected from a poet weakened in Coleridge as he grew older is to accept an unfounded legend. On the contrary, Coleridge's feelings became so powerful that they would not be restricted to a single individual, nor would they be contained within or expressed by superficial analogies with external nature, the various "toys" of thought. He was well aware that feelings cluster around an image, but he also knew that physical imagery, like the early stage of an evolving organism, must be cast aside before Being can emerge as itself, substantial and not illusory. His own poetic evolution moves away from the "concrete," the particular, the individual—elements that most modern readers expect to find in poems. Empirical criteria cannot but hinder our understanding of a poet who could write: "the more *Feeling* & less *Image*, the more substance yet the less Individuality" (CN,III,4068). Critics who remain unaware of Coleridge's intensification of feeling tend to disparage his later poems: "safely harbored at Highgate from gusts of emotion, Coleridge slowly lost the capacity to feel his disappointments intensely. Since he continued to employ the confessional mode, these late poems enact a relatively empty ritual."[4] But Coleridge's late poems are hardly "confessional," as we use that term today. In his attempt to create a new mode of poetry, a poetry of Being, the poet felt compelled to reject illustrative metaphor because it could but compromise his intensely personal needs. In his quest for what he called his "unborrow'd Self," the poet had to steer a course between the Scylla and Charybdis of mere abstraction and mere image. In the realm of pure Being, both were Phantoms.

Coleridge had already shown his readers that it was through symbol, not through metaphor, that the correspondence of the metaphysical and the physical must be dramatized. However, as early as *The Ancient Mariner*, the poet encountered a response that indicated that his audience was not yet ready to accept his "rendering the Act itself" (AR,199). The albatross had either been viewed as a physical thing, leading to the partial truth that the poem deals with man's relationship to external nature; or it had been seen exclusively as a metaphor, which Coleridge once called "a fragment of an allegory" (MC,28).[5] The latter view ignored the life outside the mind and led to the absurd conclusion that the Mariner murdered a concept. Coleridge believed that words as well as things have their own life, their own *selves*, and a symbol is the only means of declaring life, since it is neither an idea nor an image anchored in "the meanness of matter." When the poet saw the inner life, the self, the Being of that Hawk's unnameable dropping, he recognized what the Mariner should have seen in the albatross but only later learned to see in water snakes:

[4] Max F. Schulz, *The Poetic Voices of Coleridge* (Detroit: Wayne State University Press, 1964), p. 148.

[5] To express spiritual truths Coleridge chose the term "analogy" and subordinated the illustrative "metaphor" (AR,198-200). Perhaps he saw the *logos* in the Greek *analogos*.

O happy living things! no tongue
Their beauty might declare.

The Mariner's sin was what R. G. Collingwood called a "corruption of consciousness"[6] and not some mistake to be corrected by a moral lesson. Coleridge's early poem, like most of his later ones, had found its form as a fragment of a continuing process of physical and spiritual growth. The arbitrary assertion of the return to community as a "conclusion" was inappropriate because the Mariner's experience did not "declare" it. Meaning had been imposed, not discovered.

When the poet came to write "Phantom," he was able to subdue his "Understanding" and its desire to impose Procrustean conclusions. Translucence, the light of Being declaring itself through the image, could only be achieved by a language that did not dominate experience, one whose ends were not determined by conceptual logic.[7] Even when Coleridge is dealing with philosophical concepts, his remarks always have some relevance to his constant preoccupation with a language for poetry: "Preserve the pure Reason pure—& debase it not by any mixture of *sens*uality—the sensuous Imagination. To consecrate & worship the eternal distinction between the Noumenon & the Phænomenon/ and never to merge the former in the latter" (CN,III,3293). This uncompromising position might seem to undermine the poet's definition of "symbol," which "partakes of the reality it renders intelligible," but Coleridge characteristically avoids a fixed identity that would preclude dynamic interaction. The very life of the symbol is revealed in its ability to combine polarities without neutralizing them. When discussing the relationship of body and soul, Cole-

---

[6] R. G. Collingwood, *The Principles of Art* (New York: Oxford University Press, Galaxy, 1958), p. 338.

[7] I concur with Donald Davie that "the poet stands with the grammarian against the logician." Donald Davie, *Articulate Energy* (London: Routledge & Kegan Paul, 1955), p. 69.

ridge tries to keep symbol and image from merging and becoming purely sensory:

> The body,
> Eternal Shadow of the finite Soul,
> The Soul's self-symbol, its image of itself.
> Its own yet not itself.
>
> (PW,II,1001)

Thus, we can see why "translucence" was a significant word in Coleridge's vocabulary: Sara's Being that shines "through her body visibly" resembles "the soul's translucence thro' her crystal shrine!" (PW,I,455). Being is not a Platonic form; neither is it confined within a material prison. The poet must relentlessly struggle to keep his language truly "substantial." Words can remain words—stubborn, recalcitrant, bent on merging with physical objects—or they can become living things, corresponding to ideas and capable of accommodating divine light. Because Coleridge's general theory of organicism embraced words and language, he early sought to "destroy the old antithesis of *Words* & *Things*, elevating, as it were, words into Things, & living Things too" (CL,I,626). He could not bear the thought of the letter divorced from the spirit, as his qualifier "living" indicates. His idea of life required the existence of a life-giver, but Coleridge was never able to translate the Christian incarnation into a truly satisfying language for poetry. Many years later, still laboring for precision, he wrote that "Words correspond to Thoughts" (CL,VI,630), and not to things. The man's faith and the poet's language remained unfixable and ever-changing, and in his recurring dark moments, Coleridge could doubt even the metaphoric accuracy of "translucence," finding himself in a Phantom world where words had become only "impulses of air":

Words—what are they but a subtle *matter*? and the meanness of Matter must they have, & the Soul must

pine in them, even as the Lover who can press kisses
only [on] the garment of one indeed beloved. . . .
(CN,II,2998)

Although Coleridge did not give the name "Phantom" to
his lines, the poem is concerned, as we have seen, with one
of the poet's recurring problems: how to state the relationship between Being and Becoming. By setting Sara's pure,
shining Being against an outgrown physical world characterized by change and "accident," Coleridge is acknowledging that the Phantom world of shifting appearances must be
confronted and moved through rather than ignored. Like
the Eddy-pool, a Phantom must be seen before its counterfeit nature can be exposed and man can begin to evolve toward substantial Being. Coleridge believed that man began
to approach God when he refused to accept human limitations and instead, cultivated "a mind purified from the
intrusive phantoms of space and time" (LR,III,118). We
must pass through experience, and as we do so we leave
behind spiritual debris—in Coleridge's case, fragments of
poetry. If the poet in "Phantom" is able to *realize* a rare
vision of Being, unhampered by time, space, and the anchor
of sensory images, we discover him in a later poem, "Phantom or Fact," dramatizing his more common condition:
wavering between imagined purity and the day-to-day suffering of sin and alienation. In "Phantom" he was able to
conceive of a spirit liberated from confining form, but the
"lovely form" of "Phantom or Fact," although "so pure
from earthly leaven," has re-entered the world of corruption and change. Clearly, Coleridge's own guilt, which he
could never fathom, often denies him that transcendent state
which he could imagine only by way of others: Sara Hutchinson in "Dejection: An Ode" and "Phantom," and his son
Hartley in "Frost at Midnight." The poet remained most
often on the border of such transcendence, in limbo, or as
he put it, "on the threshold of some Joy, that cannot be
entered into while I am embodied" (CN,III,3370).

## Phantom or Fact
### A Dialogue in Verse
#### Author

A lovely form there sate beside my bed,
And such a feeding calm its presence shed,
A tender love so pure from earthly leaven,
That I unnethe the fancy might control,
'Twas my own spirit newly come from heaven,
Wooing its gentle way into my soul!
But ah! the change—It had not stirr'd, and yet—
Alas! that change how fain would I forget!
That shrinking back, like one that had mistook!
That weary, wandering, disavowing look!
'Twas all another, feature, look, and frame,
And still, methought, I knew, it was the same!

#### Friend

This riddling tale, to what does it belong?
Is't history? vision? or an idle song?
Or rather say at once, within what space
Of time this wild disastrous change took place?

#### Author

Call it a moment's work (and such it seems)
This tale's a fragment from the life of dreams;
But say, that years matur'd the silent strife,
And 'tis a record from the dream of life.

(PW,1,484-85)

Just as Coleridge was unable to consummate his marriage with the "lovely form" in "Phantom or Fact," he was also unable to give a conventional poetic form to his experience; he could provide only "A Dialogue in Verse." Neither could he finally resolve the question implicit in his title. How could an authentic form be appropriate to his unauthentic Being? In the limbo of his dreams, the poet is uncertain about everything. Has he encountered an apparition or a substantial Being? Is his own soul a permanent entity or some shifting appearance? Has his poetic life produced a counterfeit reality ("the life of dreams"), or has it been his means of discovering ultimate Being ("the dream of life")? Coleridge's equivocal experience alone is real, and paradox provides the avenue through which meaning can enter his life. Both "Phantom" and "Phantom or Fact" are fragments of life that are also fragments of art: powerful records that document the process of living. The Friend who attempts to elicit meaning from the Author in "Phantom or Fact" is like the wedding guest in *The Ancient Mariner*, who must acquire his living secondhand. Using his limited tools of understanding, the Friend resembles some of Coleridge's critics, or indeed any literary critic more concerned with genre than with what a form reveals; more concerned with definition than living; more concerned with the "phantoms" of time and space than with immeasurable Being:

> This riddling tale, to what does it belong?
> Is't history? vision? or an idle song?
> Or rather say at once, within what space
> Of time this wild disastrous change took place?

In his attempt to categorize, the Friend has missed the underlying reality of the experience, and he appears more desperately frantic in his questioning than the Author, who accepts the balanced uncertainty of paradox. Evading the limits of conventional naming, Coleridge calls his work a "fragment" or a "record."

Since Coleridge's dreams, as his notebooks and letters show, were more terrifyingly real to him than many of the events of his waking life, the "shrinking back" of his better self in "Phantom or Fact" makes the poet realize that he himself may be the Phantom. The poem could as well have been called "Phantom *and* Fact," since each has a validating power in the poet's reverie. With the perspective gained in his old age, Coleridge viewed his dreams as "having been in fact the worst Realities of my life" (CL,vi,767).[8] He knew that the abstract thought he had entertained in order to alleviate his anguish had been perhaps his most formidable Phantom because it produced, in Kierkegaard's words, a "thought without a thinker."[9] Coleridge's preference for experience over ideas about experience was evident in his objection to the Deists who "imposed upon themselves an *Idea* for a Reality: a most sublime Idea indeed, and so necessary to human Nature, that without it no Virtue is conceivable; but still an Idea!" (AR,136). When the poet's Friend-Critic asks whether the Author has attempted to convey "history" or "vision," he betrays his limited awareness of possibility. Coleridge has, in effect, achieved all of the categories about which the Friend queries him: a riddling tale, personal history, vision, and an idle (self-circling, like an idler wheel), inconclusive song.

The imaginative conflict that Coleridge presents in "Phantom or Fact" can be seen as another example of the poet's attempt to give "living" meaning to the words with which he expresses his struggle for Being. As with most of his later poetry, this poem seeks a formal marriage of idea and fact, having found each in isolation to be a distortion of reality. Such poetic marriage would eventually be sanctified by a religion that also "must consist of ideas and facts both; not of ideas alone without facts, for then it would be mere Philosophy;—nor of facts alone without ideas of which those facts are the symbols, or out of which they arise, or upon which they are grounded, for then it would be mere History" (TT,ii,13). Coleridge's choice was not between

[8] He also expressed the same thought earlier: "dreams are no Shadows with me; but the real, substantial miseries of Life" (CL,ii,986).

[9] Søren Kierkegaard, *Concluding Unscientific Postscript*, trans. David F. Swenson and Walter Lowrie (London: Oxford University Press, 1941), p. 296.

extremes, rather it was a choice of the area where "extremes meet," a comprehensive vision in which the "life of dreams" and the "dream of life" continually meet in an act of redefinition. Based on Coleridge's temporal experience, "Phantom or Fact" seeks to give personal history the translucence of Christian history. Without fact, as Coleridge uses the word, all life is but an illusion or shadow, and man but "a phantom dim of past and future wrought" (PW,I,487). However, like mere philosophy and mere history, "how mean a thing a mere fact is, except as seen in the light of some comprehensive truth" (*Friend*,I,358). Facts for Coleridge, do not possess the solidity of empirical data; they are only aspects of an evolving form, materials continually being *transformed*. What Owen Barfield writes should serve as a warning to readers of Coleridge's poetry and perhaps to readers of Romantic poetry in general: "For the pure prosaic can apprehend nothing but *results*. It knows nought of the thing coming into being, only of the thing become. It cannot realize *shapes*. It sees nature—and would like to see art—as a series of mechanical rearrangements of *facts*. And facts are *facta*—things done and past."[10] In "Phantom or Fact," the "silent strife" of poetic meditation clears the way for the arrival of Being. The inconclusive conclusion of this fragment testifies not to Coleridge's inability as a maker, but to his comprehensive vision of form which subordinated poetry to Being.

Near the end of his meditative *Aids to Reflection*, Coleridge makes some remarks that serve aptly as a gloss for "Phantom" and "Phantom or Fact," as well as for the poet's use of "Phantom" in general. Words such as "translucence," "facts," "silent strife," "Spectres and Apparitions," and "dream," indicate an obsessive area of concern:

> The translucence, of the invisible Energy, which soon surrenders or abandons them to inferior Powers. . . .

[10] Owen Barfield, *Poetic Diction: A Study in Meaning* (Middletown, Conn.: Wesleyan University Press, 1972), pp. 168-169.

These are not fancies, conjectures, or even hypotheses, but *facts*; to deny which is impossible, not to reflect on which is ignominious. And we need only reflect on them with a calm and silent spirit to learn the utter emptiness and unmeaningness of the vaunted Mechanico-corpuscular Philosophy, with both its twins, Materialism on the one hand, and Idealism, rightlier named *Subjective Idolism*, on the other: the one obtruding on us as a World of Spectres and Apparitions; the other a mazy Dream. (AR,391)

His twins, materialism and idealism, are Phantoms because as fixed concepts they ignore the fact that knowledge is an alternating current running between two poles, and illuminating the life it cannot define. Each of Coleridge's poems may appear to be "a moment's work" only because we fail to realize the continuum out of which it arises; it is not a self-sustaining object, but a fragment *from* life, an outlet for "the invisible Energy." Coleridge would never abandon himself to a poem, and the ending of "Phantom or Fact," like the ending of Keats's "Ode to a Nightingale," refuses to present a solid, static picture of reality. After accepting the failure of visionary escape ("Fled is that vision") Keats returns to his own "invisible Energy" which is constantly seeking a form for itself: "Do I wake or sleep?" Like Keats, Coleridge momentarily incorporates into his poem the dream of life, the life of dream, and further, the life *in* dream. After suggesting a possible meaning ("Call it a moment's work"), Coleridge undermines his own tentative definition with a qualifying "But say." Language, both poems seem to assert, can make only ambiguous declarations of Being. But Being is not ambiguous.

As long as Coleridge could participate in the life of dream, and avoid the Phantom life of nightmare, he could endure the "silent strife" necessary to keep him from losing consciousness and falling into non-Being. But a Phantom could become a more terrifying spectre, a diabolical force energized by a corrupted will. Dream and nightmare were to be carefully distinguished, but, like the productive and the destructive Eddy, one could suddenly turn into the other. Dream is productive when it allows the subconscious to originate form, and when, through a "suspension of will and the comparative power" (ShC,I,129), the part of a poet's life that is *in* dreams can emerge and find its "outness." Coleridge does not suggest that poets assume a totally passive role in dealing with their dreams, just as he rejected Wordsworth's "wise passiveness" before the natural world. Sleep can swamp the will and reduce man to an animal state that lacks all form. Coleridge's consciously made fragments never seem like random collisions within animal sleep. For the poet maintains a crucial distinction between the suspension of will brought about by natural processes and the "willing suspension of disbelief" that should be the act of both creative artist and creative reader. The artist chooses to deceive; the reader chooses to be deceived. Like the forceful acts of reflection and comparison, Coleridge's suspension of the mind was a powerful act in which the human will worked from *motives*, and not from mere "dark instincts" (*Friend*,I,160). It follows that reverie, or "halfsleep," was a more desirable state than sleep, because in the zone between sleeping and waking man's judgment could be on guard against the deceptions of Phantoms. Dream or reverie could produce congenial Phantoms (if not Wordsworth's "Phantom of delight"), and the semi-conscious Coleridge could enjoy the role of psychoanalyst as he tracked images to their sources, trying to understand his motives and the "working of the mind."

The nightmare—or night-mair as Coleridge sometimes spelled it—was the daydream or nightdream gone mad: the poet's dark instincts turned loose to conspire with the phenomenal world and produce Phantoms of fear and dread. As with the negative face of the Eddy image, the nightmare revealed the self out of control. One notebook entry, already cited in connection with "Dejection: An Ode," unites Eddy with nightmare: "whirled about without a center—as in a nightmair—no gravity—a vortex without a center" (CN,III,3999). Because Coleridge's Phantoms assumed an actual existence, the poet associated the Phantom with language and considered both as manifestations of the material world. Even when the poet describes what might be his opium dreams, we can often sense that he is dealing with poetic problems as well as physiological ones, as in these lines from the early "Ode to the Departing Year":

> The Voice had ceas'd, the Vision fled;
> Yet still I gasp'd and reel'd with dread.
> And ever, when the dream of night
> Renews the phantom to my sight,
> Cold sweat-drops gather on my limbs
>
> (PW,I,166)

Reeling with dread, the poet cannot free himself from his Phantom world where things are only things, and poems are only images of things. However, because the spectre is not *ultimately* real, the poet must overpower it and move toward the synthesis of Being and Becoming that is shown in the poem "Phantom." He must free himself from the body and restore life to words-as-*facta*. Substance is not what is seen, just as the poem is not truly on the page.

An exchange from his play *Remorse* may help to clarify Coleridge's use of both "Phantom" and "Substance," and to show how he questions the customary meanings of words. Teresa, believing her husband Alver to be dead, appears before Ordonio:

> *Ordonio*:  Teresa? or the phantom of Teresa?
> *Teresa*:  Alas! the phantom only, if in truth
>      The substance of her being, her life's life,
>      Have ta'en its flight through Alvar's death-wound.
>
> (PW,II,855-56)

Ordonio is asking, in effect, are you a Phantom or a fact? Her reply defines both a natural and a poetic process: Teresa demonstrates that Being, or "life's life," transforms superficial form. The Phantom is what one struggles against, what one leaves behind. And for Coleridge this Phantom was death—or arrested development, death-in-life. As the poet wrote in *The Friend*, "What we have within, that only can we see without. I cannot *see* death: and he that hath not this freedom is a slave. He is in the arms of that, the phantom of which he beholdeth and seemeth to himself to flee from" (*Friend*,1,411). Coleridge knew that if he could keep his reason awake then he would not experience such terrifying dread. The problem may have been intensified by the poet's opium addiction, but it had existed long before. For example, a letter of 1794 describes "some horrible phantom" that threatens him but disappears when confronted. As a youth of twenty-two, Coleridge knew the power of will over matter: "even so will the greater part of our mental Miseries vanish before an Effort. Whatever of mind we *will* do, we *can* do" (CL,1,123). However, the Phantom was not so easily subdued as Coleridge thought, and the struggle became, in its most painful stage, an unending "war-embrace of wrestling life and death" (PW,1,394).

During a nightmare, sensations would be mingled with forms created not by the conscious will, but by the imagination. And Coleridge felt that reason should be the agent to rescue the emerging dream-life images from the sea of the unconscious: "the power of Reason being in good measure awake, most generally presents to us all the accompanying images very nearly as they existed the moment before, when we fell out of anxious wakefulness into this *Reverie*" (CN,111,4046). The poet is specifically discussing poetry here, but the terms he employs as he continues—"senses," "form," "images," "imagination," "the true inward Creatrix"—suggest the underlying singleness of purpose throughout Coleridge's writing. A poem could be a record of a dream, a product of reverie or of that "species of Reverie" called nightmare, but it could never *be* a dream. Rather, "a poem may in one sense be a dream, but it must be a waking dream" (MC,162). In "Kubla Khan" the poet's imagination could summon up disparate images, but some reasoning power had to order them, and this power had to come from within. The poem was labeled in 1816, seventeen or eighteen years after its composition, "A Vision in a Dream." Coleridge, by this time, was able to articulate with more certainty that the "stupor" of his "external senses" had allowed images to rise up "as *things*," and that such images were "accompanied by *words*." However, this does not mean that the act of *making* the poem was in any way irrational. The note, after all, questions whether the experience of a dream "can be called composition," and the author points out that "on awaking he appeared to himself to have a distinct recollection." The poet's insistence that "reason can exert no influence" during reverie, and his equally firm assertion that reason must be "in good measure awake" before a dream experience can become art, should alert us to the precise meanings with which Coleridge endows his carefully chosen language: the poet was *awake* and he only *appeared* to remember.

In the celebrated "Kubla Khan," the conflict between Phantom dream associations and willed poetic form reaches a point of reconciliation, even though the poem seems incoherent to some readers. As Humphrey House pointed out, we would probably never have considered the poem a fragment without the poet's note warning us in advance that our expectations would not be fulfilled. In order to appreciate Coleridge's art, we cannot discount his own analysis of his creative act by considering it distorted or self-justifying. Asleep, one is at the mercy of primordial chaos; completely awake, one denies oneself the possibility of subliminal power. Images are only materials, phantoms to be brought under control. And just as a poem is a fragment from the poet's life, Coleridge believed, so the universe is an "unfolded fragment of the Deity" (CN,II,3088). Poems are important not for what they are, but for what they tell us about Being. They too become Phantoms when we treat them as ends, as aesthetic objects that exist only for this world. In his final decade, Coleridge remains alert to the continuing threat of materialism and fixed form:

> No apprehension can be turned into a Certainty, no *Thought* returned upon us a *Thing*, without a sad'ning Suddenness that for the moment lays our powers prostrate & which no fore-bodings, however distinct, no not prescience itself can disarm of it's sting or blunt it's sharpness.—But let the Thing settle back & thin away again, into a Thought—& the Evil shrinks with it into human & bearable Dimensions. (CL,v,503)

Art could not be for Coleridge, as it could not be for Blake, a logical, Urizenic petrifaction of reality. We can apply our intellect to "Kubla Khan," but if we only concentrate on the poem's external shape we are no better than the poet's Friend in "Phantom or Fact":

> This riddling tale, to what does it belong?
> Is't history? vision? or an idle song?

The Author's reply serves for most of Coleridge's poems:

> Call it a moment's work (and such it seems)
> This tale's a fragment from the life of dreams.

Whether it was the "one life" or the "one spirit" that transfigured Sara's bodily form in "Phantom," Coleridge was seeking to bring coherence to Being, not to art. By calling his poems fragments, he was directing his readers to the true "substance" beyond the Phantom appearance of perfected form.

Like Blake, Coleridge saw through and not with his eye, and as we have seen, his distrust of "picture language" and "idols of sense" created difficulties in finding a consummate metaphor for Being. A couple of years before writing "Phantom," the poet had already conducted an epistemological experiment in which he considered the limitations of representational art. In "The Picture," both external nature and art are exposed as phantoms of Being, one a "watery idol," the other a "relique" which can only testify to a life that has already moved on. In this lighthearted poem (almost a *jeu d'esprit*) that belies its serious concerns, Coleridge assumes a dual role so that he may bring into play his attitudes toward "nature poetry" and the poetic myths by which man attempts to integrate himself with his earthly surroundings.[11] By creating two voices, "I" and "He," the poet can objectify his own conflicts as thinker and poet in his daily struggle for Unity of Being. As in his later poem "Constancy to an Ideal Object," the "He" indicates a man who is the victim of illusions about nature:

> The enamoured rustic worships its fair hues,
> Nor knows he makes the shadow, he pursues!

In contrast, the "I" becomes the poet who needs to have his inchoate feelings guided into some conscious, tangible form. Self-irony is Coleridge's means of recognizing his own Phantoms. Wishing to be free of his need for human companionship, the "I" wanders in "romantic" fashion ("I know not, ask not whither"), careless of whether nature is a guide or simply a playmate. However, by the end of the poem, Coleridge has redefined his own "passion" and found the "resolution" to pursue it. Realizing the inadequacy of his love *object* ("full of love to all, save only me"), he discovers that the pursuit of Being, the possibility of apprehending Being, supersedes any sense object. In Coleridge's terms, impulse has been educated into motive, as the following excerpt from "The Picture" demonstrates:

> Sweet breeze! thou only, if I guess aright,
> Liftest the feathers of the robin's breast,
> That swells its little breast, so full of song,
> Singing above me, on the mountain-ash.
> And thou too, desert stream! no pool of thine,
> Though clear as lake in latest summer-eve,
> Did e'er reflect the stately virgin's robe,
> The face, the form divine, the downcast look

---

[11] Concerning "The Picture" Coleridge said, "I disguised my own sensations" (CL,III,499).

Contemplative! Behold! her open palm
Presses her cheek and brow! her elbow rests
On the bare branch of half-uprooted tree,
That leans towards its mirror! Who erewhile
Had from her countenance turned, or looked by stealth,
(For Fear is true-love's cruel nurse), he now
With steadfast gaze and unoffending eye,
Worships the watery idol, dreaming hopes
Delicious to the soul, but fleeting, vain,
E'en as that phantom-world on which he gazed,
But not unheeded gazed: for see, ah! see,
The sportive tyrant with her left hand plucks
The heads of tall flowers that behind her grow,
Lychnis, and willow-herb, and fox-glove bells:
And suddenly, as one that toys with time,
Scatters them on the pool! Then all the charm
Is broken—all that phantom world so fair
Vanishes, and a thousand circlets spread,
And each mis-shape the other. Stay awhile,
Poor youth, who scarcely dar'st lift up thine eyes!
The stream will soon renew its smoothness, soon
The visions will return! And lo! he stays:
And soon the fragments dim of lovely forms
Come trembling back, unite, and now once more
The pool becomes a mirror; and behold
Each wildflower on the marge inverted there,
And there the half-uprooted tree—but where,
O where the virgin's snowy arm, that leaned
On its bare branch? He turns, and she is gone!
Homeward she steals through many a woodland maze
Which he shall seek in vain. Ill-fated youth!
Go, day by day, and waste thy manly prime
In mad love-yearning by the vacant brook,
Till sickly thoughts bewitch thine eyes, and thou
Behold'st her shadow still abiding there,
The Naiad of the mirror!

(PW,1,369-74,11.68-111)

63

In earlier sections of "The Picture," before the lines just quoted, Coleridge could be satirizing all nature lovers (including Wordsworth) who "worship the spirit of unconscious life," aspiring to lose their Being by becoming "something that [they know] not of,/ In winds or waters, or among the rocks!" Coleridge not only rejects nature as a self-fulfilling object, he rejects the pagan myths that personify it. In a bantering tone, the poet refuses to use Cupid as the name or picture for his passion, announcing that "His little Godship" could not survive in a real world: "low stumps shall gore/ His dainty feet." And even in places where he sounds like the early Keats, who would retreat into the "green recessed woods" and be safe from "all breathing human passion," Coleridge leaves room for his criticism of another Phantom, the "theory of association" whereby a physical object can summon up feelings that overpower the human will:

> love-distempered youth,
> Who ne'er henceforth may see an aspen-grove
> Shiver in sunshine, but his feeble heart
> Shall flow away like a dissolving thing.

Coleridge's role throughout the poem is to "play the merry fool," while at the same time seriously considering some avenues of escape for man when he is unfulfilled by a human love object: escape into nature, into art, into hedonism. And yet Coleridge is never deceived by his own images. Looking back on "The Picture" in later life, he continues to define his lover's sickness as "the relaxing Malaria of the Mystic Divinity, which affects to languish after an extinction of individual Consciousness—the sickly state which I had myself described [in "The Picture"]" (CL,vi,555).

By distinguishing the conscious "I" from the fanciful "He," who is deceived by his image in nature's pool, the poet can acknowledge his own youthful desire "to project this phantom-world into the world of Reality . . . to make ideas & realities stand side by side, the one as vivid as the

other" (CL,II,1000). Within the pool of language that becomes this poem, Coleridge can discover an *image* of himself, just as the "gentle lunatic" sees his lover in a stream.
However, unlike Narcissus, Coleridge knows that any
image, as a representation or picture of the body, is inferior
both to the body and ultimately to Being, the life within
that informs the body. Both the Narcissus and Echo myths
end in death, since neither figure is able to consummate his
desire. But Coleridge can use his self-reflection as a means
to redirect his passion toward "a world of Reality." Narcissus fell in love with Coleridge's Phantom, a shadow (the
myth reads *spem sine corpore amat, corpus putat esse, quod
umbra est*), and Narcissus' failure to distinguish appearance
from reality is the primary flaw in Coleridge's "love-distem-
pered youth," who is "sick in soul" and is a "gentle lunatic"
suffering from "mad love-yearning" and "sickly thoughts."
When illusion degenerates into delusion, no evolution of
consciousness, no movement toward Being, is possible. By
imaginatively *playing* the "Merry fool," the poet suspends
his own disbelief but he never succumbs to natural tempta-
tions. Both early and late in his poetic life, Coleridge was
alert to the dangers of identifying Being with its phenomenal reflection, its non-living appearances in physical things
and words as things.[12] In *Aids to Reflection*, he wrote:

> Shall his [man's] pursuits and desires, the *reflexions* of
> his inward life, be like the reflected Image of a Tree
> on the edge of a Pool, that grows downward, and seeks
> a mock heaven in the unstable element beneath it, in

[12] In revising "Frost at Midnight" Coleridge interpolated these
lines:

> Whose puny flaps and freaks the idling Spirit
> By its own moods interprets, every where
> Echo or Mirror seeking of itself,
> And makes a toy of Thought.

True self-reflection is finally independent of any reflection from
physical nature which only diverts us from our Being, "makes a toy
of Thought."

neighbourhood with the slim water-weeds and oozy bottom-grass that are yet better than itself and more noble, in as far as Substances that appear as Shadows are preferable to Shadows mistaken for Substances. (AR,-112)

As his poem "Phantom or Fact" demonstrates, however, Coleridge spent a great deal of his life in that zone where Substance and Shadow meet, where Being cannot be indicated except through paradox. In "The Picture," he again divided himself in the hope of forging a new consciousness of Being. By accepting the consolation of nature and art, the "fragments dim of lovely forms," Coleridge's "He" is left in a state of waste and vacancy, waiting for a phantom that resides in a phantom. But the poet's "I" recognizes the futility of finding any permanent house for the "form divine," although like Orpheus, he steals a look at bodily form ("eye-poisons"), aware that he is "plucking the poisons of self-harm." For Coleridge, the myth of Narcissus probably indicated the failure of visual imagery to define Being. Both the poet's persona and Narcissus come to nature in order to escape human passion, and ironically, both discover that their passion has only been sublimated. But whereas Narcissus falls in love with the picture of what he seeks, Coleridge, after rejecting the abiding "Naiad of the mirror," continues to pursue his "form divine." By doing so, Coleridge suggests that a progressive realization of Being can never be achieved by contemplating the Phantom world.

The remainder of "The Picture" traces the progress of the pilgrim who has resisted the sirens of sense and art but still believes himself free of human passion. He has discovered what nature is *not*—it is not a dead end—but he has still to discover what it can *be*. As he sets forth, he is accompanied by an instinctual "joy,/ Lovely as light" that he is unable to locate or define with any certainty: it "beckons me on, or follows from behind,/ Playmate, or guide." After emerging from the shadows, he again encounters light, but now it is not self-generated or seen reflected in a pool, but is an active energy declaring its Being within and through nature. Just as man's Being cannot be found reflected in a passive pool, so nature's Being is not "the dead Shapes, the outward *Letter*—but the Life of Nature revealing itself in the Phaenomenon, or rather attempting to reveal itself" (CL,IV,607). The poet provides more than natural description in the scene in which the youth is rescued from his own self-indulgence:

> How fair the sunshine spots that mossy rock,
> Isle of the river, whose disparted waves
> Dart off asunder with an angry sound,
> How soon to re-unite! And see! they meet,
> Each in the other lost and found: and see
> Placeless, as spirits, one soft water-sun
> Throbbing within them, heart at once and eye!

In contrast to the "Eye-poisons" of sensual pleasures, this is Being itself, an energy "throbbing within" that must remain "placeless," and beyond any secondary representation. Since language linked with Understanding cannot describe a supersensual experience, the poet can but celebrate the natural opposites that continually "reunite," evoking the "peace that passeth all understanding": "I pass forth into light."

Although Coleridge's poem abounds in descriptive detail, it seeks to direct the self's evolution upward toward idea, not downward toward physical image. When, following his moment of epiphany, the speaker fortuitously discovers the "Picture" (the art object of the poem's title), he knows now that he must look beyond its superficial form if he is to be fulfilled. His human affections summon up that which is contained in the art object: the light of creating power. Consequently, the speaker realizes what Narcissus failed to see: that representation is not Being, and that passion directed toward the phenomenal self produces a destructive Phantom. The poem ends:

67

> Why should I yearn
> To keep the relique? 'twill but idly feed
> The passion that consumes me. Let me haste!
> The picture in my hand that she has left;
> She cannot blame me that I followed her:
> And I may be her guide the long wood through.

The poet has encountered and overcome his passive self, and has discovered the light "throbbing within" images, a view that "bursts" upon the sight. The energy within nature corresponds to the energy within man. Rather than remaining mesmerized by nature's pool, in which desire can never be consummated, the speaker wills himself toward his ideal self which is always in the process of being attained. The mirror images of both nature and art are Phantoms. Although "The Picture" ends on a prospective note, as do most of Coleridge's poems, nature has been the poet's means of restoring energy to hope and power to his suspended reason.

Seeming to deny Aristotle's antithesis of art and nature, Coleridge considered both as evocations of the "life" that is continually shaping itself. Like nature, a poem can have no end because:

> An ultimate end must of necessity be an idea, that is, that which is not representable by the sense, and has no entire correspondent in nature, or the world of the senses. For in nature there can be neither a first nor a last:—all that we can see, smell, taste, touch, are means, and only in a qualified sense, and by the defect of our language, entitled ends. (Shedd,v,514)

The poet must shatter icons of conventional form (Coleridge called himself "Idoloclastes Satyrane" in his poem "A Tombless Epitaph") in order to release substantial Being. Coleridge's fragments, like those of Eliot later, may indicate "an extreme cohesion of thought."[13] Because neither poet

[13] Thomas McFarland, *Coleridge and the Pantheist Tradition* (Oxford: Clarendon Press, 1969), p. xxxvii. Although Professor McFarland's book ostensibly deals only with philosophical ideas, it reveals a deep understanding of Coleridge's struggle with poetic form.

was content with the apparent Being of the world, neither was satisfied with a representative *picture* of objects. Both were supremely capable of making shapes, but both suffered a duality that could not be permanently healed by simple means. They both turned inward and, in their stages of spiritual growth, moved steadily away from dependence on the natural world and metaphor as illustration. Poetry itself can be a Phantom when it diverts us from consciousness of ultimate Being.

Once Coleridge decided that the physical world was often an untrustworthy Phantom, he felt obligated to expose the logic of the human "Understanding" by which men attempt to deduce meaning and value from unsubstantial appearances. His poem "Human Life" is sometimes misread as a revelation of his personal despair, whereas, in truth, it is about his confrontation with despair: the poet lets his spectre speak, and allows his own understanding to pursue its "phantom purposes" by beginning with a faulty premise and relentlessly and logically moving toward nihilism and schizophrenia. Hope and "substantial" faith in immortality belong to the poet who controls the poem's movement. But since they are ignored by his limited persona, they must remain outside the language which, after the initial doubting "If," becomes itself a "shadow" of the "shadowy self." An awareness of Coleridge's definitions of "Life" and "Phantom" helps us to detect the poet's irony, which is his means of directing us toward his true subject: a belief in immortality that makes speculation absurd.

### Human Life
#### [Contemplated] On the Denial of Immortality

If dead, we cease to be; if total gloom
    Swallow up life's brief flash for aye, we fare
As summer-gusts, of sudden birth and doom,
    Whose sound and motion not alone declare,
But are their whole of being! If the breath
    Be Life itself, and not its task and tent,

If even a soul like Milton's can know death;
  O Man! thou vessel purposeless, unmeant,
Yet drone-hive strange of phantom purposes!
  Surplus of Nature's dread activity,
Which, as she gazed on some nigh-finished vase,
Retreating slow, with meditative pause,
  She formed with restless hands unconsciously.
Blank accident! nothing's anomaly!
If rootless thus, thus substanceless thy state,
Go, weigh thy dreams, and be thy hopes, thy fears,
The counter-weights!—Thy laughter and thy tears
  Mean but themselves, each fittest to create
And to repay the other! Why rejoices
  Thy heart with hollow joy for hollow good?
Why cowl thy face beneath the mourner's hood?
Why waste thy sighs, and thy lamenting voices,
  Image of Image, Ghost of Ghostly Elf,
That such a thing as thou feel'st warm or cold?
Yet what and whence thy gain, if thou withhold
  These costless shadows of thy shadowy self?
Be sad! be glad! be neither! seek, or shun!
Thou hast no reason why! Thou canst have none;
Thy being's being is contradiction.

(PW,1,425-26)

George Watson, misunderstanding the poet's method, concludes that "positive negation" may be for Coleridge "the best that life offers,"[14] And James Boulger's reading seems questionable when he emphasizes only a portion of the title: "Denial of Immortality."[15] Coleridge's critics are

[14] George Watson, *Coleridge the Poet* (London: Routledge & Kegan Paul, 1966), p. 136.

[15] James Boulger, *Coleridge as Religious Thinker* (New Haven: Yale University Press, 1961), p. 208. The title for the version in *Philosophical Lectures* more strongly emphasizes the speculative nature of the poem: "Human life contemplated on the denial of Immortality" (PL,211). In *Sibylline Leaves* (1817) the poem is subtitled "A Fragment." In a recent selection of Coleridge's poems, the full

sometimes deceived by the Phantoms that the poet exorcises, for Coleridge was not suffering "the breakdown of spirit and matter in the old immanential unity";[16] rather, he assumes an absurd position in order to prove a sound one. The initial "If," and the others that follow it, bring into play a whole series of falsehoods. Therefore the meaning of the poem can never be deduced from the Phantom evidence presented, and deliberately so. Coleridge wrote: "why do you fly off from the facts to a gigantic fiction,— when the possibility of the *If* with respect to a much less startling narration is the point in dispute between us?" (Shedd,v,437). Believing that "there is no contradiction in anything but degraded man" (CN,III,3281), the poet chooses to *employ* contradictions until we can see beyond them, "till by negations we stand on the edge of a new faculty" (CN,III,3575). That new faculty is a consciousness of Being that is totally absent from the thinking process described in "Human Life," which begins in academic speculation and ends in suicidal despair. Coleridge's belief in a Supreme Being was evident in his love for the human Being. As he wrote to his friend Poole, "Love so deep & so domesticated with the whole Being, as mine was to you, can never cease *to be*" (CL,III,435). And he clearly stated that "Not *TO BE*, then, is impossible: TO BE, incomprehensible" (*Friend*,I,514).

As we have seen in connection with the Eddy metaphor, Coleridge envisioned human life as a forward-moving stream, continuous in spite of occasional eddies. Man's "natural" mind can define life only by deducing it from appearances, but the poet believes that nature provides only a dead end, that value cannot be derived from experience or, as Eliot says, there is "only a limited value/ In the knowledge

---

title is abbreviated and the subtitle eliminated: *Coleridge's Verse: A Selection*, ed. William Empson and David Pirie (London: Faber & Faber, 1972), p. 202.

[16] Boulger, *Coleridge as Religious Thinker*, p. 207.

derived from experience."[17] This "limited" human under-standing, which Coleridge recognizes as "the source and faculty of words" (PL,403), is doomed to contradiction whenever it seeks to investigate "means" in the hope of finding an "end." He wrote that "Physiologically contem-plated, Nature begins, proceeds, and ends in a contradiction; for the moment of absolute solution would be that in which Nature would cease to be Nature, i.e. a scheme of ever-varying relations" (TL,53). To see human life simply as a "surplus of Nature's dread activity" is to deprive man of his consciousness and his will to act. Wordsworth could at one time picture man passively "Rolled round in earth's diurnal course,/ With rocks, and stones, and trees," but Coleridge's use of "dread" to describe nature's act reveals his obsessive fear of being identified with matter. Death can end natural existence but it cannot end life, for, as his poem implicitly states, "the breath" is not "Life itself." The poet brings to his poem, as we must bring to our reading of it, the presumption of permanent Being. If not, we will be captivated by the poem's Phantom appearances. Coleridge confronts doubt, and pursues his negative vision in order to convince himself of its absurdity. Logic is used to unmask logic. In a notebook entry of 1817, the year the poem was published, Coleridge provides a gloss for "Human Life":

> The best proof of immortality is the fact, that the pre-sumption of it is at the bottom of every hope, fear, and action. Suppose for a moment an intuitive certainty that we should cease to be at a given time—the *Whole* feeling of futurity would be extinguished at the first feeling of such a certainty—and the mind would have no motive for not dying at the same moment.—This *must*, I know, but I likewise know, that it *may* be developed and made intelligible. (CN,III,4356)

[17] T. S. Eliot, *The Complete Poems and Plays* (New York: Har-court, Brace & Co., 1952), p. 125.

Coleridge surely has a "motive" in denying man his continuity. The thought that Being ceases with the death of the body produces a poem of "total gloom," in effect proving Blake's adage: "If the sun and moon should doubt,/ They'd immediately go out." And like Blake, Coleridge needed to resort to contradiction and paradox in order to release the energy of Being.

According to Coleridge, "contradiction"—especially "self-contradiction"—was to be avoided in every human act. But like any Phantom metaphor, it could be *used* to point toward that Unity of Being which absorbs all intellectual categories. Owen Barfield accurately comments on Coleridge's use of "contradiction":

> Now the immediate product of reason in the understanding is the principle of contradiction. But only that which itself transcends two contradictories can have produced them. Thus, if we do not remain wilfully blind, our attention is drawn, by the truth in contradiction itself to "the truths of reason." It is indeed a "test and sign" of any truth of reason that *"it can come forth out of the moulds of the understanding only in the disguise of two contradictory conceptions."*[18]

The Phantom "disguise" that Barfield discovers in Coleridge's *Aids to Reflection* troubled the poet much earlier when he was trying to imagine how his language could express the mystery of Being:

> I would make a pilgrimage to the Deserts of Arabia to find the man who could make [me] understand how the *one can be many*! Eternal universal mystery! It seems as if it were impossible; yet it *is*—& it is everywhere!— It is indeed a contradiction *in Terms*: and only in Terms!—It is the co presence of Feeling & Life, limitless by their very essence, with Form, by its very essence limited—determinate—definite. (CN,I,1561)

[18] Owen Barfield, *What Coleridge Thought* (Middletown, Conn.: Wesleyan University Press, 1971), pp. 110-11.

Being, then, cannot be defined in the terms of a depraved language,[19] and the poet's task is to affirm a new language for Being, one worthy of man's reason, a universal language for redeemed man: "whatever contradicts this universal language, therefore, contradicts the universal consciousness" (LR,I,325).

Choosing to sever his relationship to the universal consciousness with his prideful "If," the speaker of "Human Life" suffers the frustration of a man who acts when he has nothing to act *for*. Failure inevitably follows such frustration because, as Kierkegaard said, "to maintain a relationship to the absolute *telos* is no contradiction, but is the absolute correspondence of like to like. . . . Contradiction of worldly passion arises from the attempt to sustain an absolute relationship to a relative *telos*."[20] As a poet, Coleridge allows his Phantom understanding to express his own doubt, but what he doubts is the ability of natural science, natural philosophy, or natural religion to uncover authentic Being. Poetry can supply "the material of outness, *materiam objectivam*" (PL,403), but poetry, like external nature, may reflect only Phantoms of Being—an "image of an image"— as seen through Coleridge's use of the Narcissus myth in "The Picture" and elsewhere. By picturing himself as an object of nature (i.e., belonging to nature) Coleridge could probe his own anxiety in the face of ultimate Being and, in the end, expose his own "latent disbelief." As he wrote: "whether the Knowing of the Mind has its correlative in the Being of Nature, doubts may be felt. Never to have felt them, would indeed betray an unconscious unbelief, which traced to its extreme roots will be seen grounded in a latent disbelief" (*Friend*,I,512). In "Human Life" the poet allows his "*negative* faith" (BL,II,107) to lower him from "universal consciousness," dramatizing his own personal "tendency to self-contempt, a sense of the utter disproportionateness

---

[19] Coleridge commented that "language itself confesses the depravity of our nature!" (PL,421).

[20] Kierkegaard, *Concluding Unscientific Postscript*, pp. 337-38.

of all, I can call *me*, to the promises of the Gospel—*this* is *my* sorest temptation" (CL,VI,573).

This poem proceeds from its initial statement of doubt to accumulate a series of meaningless actions, "Phantom purposes" that allow Being eventually to be trapped by contradiction ("Thy being's being is contradiction"), and thus by despair. Human life is identified with natural appearances, a "brief flash" or a "summer-gust" that must eventually subside into darkness and stasis. Coleridge's entire poem laments the separation of experience from its meaning, laments that things can "mean but themselves." Just as the phenomenal sound and motion of natural creatures should reveal the energy within nature, so man's metaphors should *declare* his meaning. Coleridge's title should probably be inverted to read "Human Death: Contemplated on the Denial of Immortality"; for by perversely ignoring inner Being, the substance that "is and must be in ourselves" (BL,II,259), man becomes identified with matter, becomes an image of an image. Experiencing death-in-life, he has no *reason* not to abandon himself entirely to his Phantom world:

> Yet what and whence thy gain, if thou withhold
> These costless shadows of thy shadowy self?

The questions shaped by the understanding cannot be answered by the understanding. Coleridge's portrait of degraded man is designed to be "a deceptive counterfeit of [his] superficial form" (BL,II,65), depicting a bankrupt creature who is now ready to be filled with his identifying substance, which is not found in nature. The despair expressed in "Human Life," and other of Coleridge's later poems, seems often to be a despair that serves an eventual joyful affirmation. The poet is like the chrysalis that, through suffering, discards its Phantom, material form because this form is ultimately valueless, "these costless shadows of thy shadowy self."

Coleridge could imagine discontinuity in life, and could

in his dark hours even wish not to exist, but he never doubted his *need* for permanent Being. He refused to be a Phantom "Image of Image, Ghost of Ghostly Elf," or a passive creature that nature "formed with restless hands unconsciously." Coleridge believed in "joy" even when he could not bring it into his day-to-day life, and he found no value in natural man, considering him a form without content. His question, "Why rejoices/ Thy heart with hollow joy for hollow good?" contains its implicit answer: that there is a joy that passes all understanding and it must be sought through the "Universal Consciousness," just as Coleridge's purpose is achieved by means of "purposeless" man. In concluding another late poem, "Youth and Age," the poet composed these lines, which were not included in the published version:

> O! might *Life* cease! and selfless Mind,
> Whose total *Being* is *Act*, alone remain behind!
>
> (CL,VI,910)

The poem "Human Life" embodies an act anticipating ultimate Being, and it should probably have as its coda these words from a notebook: "N.B. The obscurity of this argument consists wholly in the impossibility of actually conceiving a discontinuity in our Being—Eternity is its Substance" (CN,III,4356).

Comparing Coleridge's "Human Life" to George Herbert's "The Collar," we realize how different the poetic forms for Christian life may be. Both poets' meditations strive to bring to natural man the knowledge of his incompleteness; but, whereas Herbert resolves the conflicts he creates, Coleridge begins and ends his poem with a troubling contradiction. Coleridge's "negative faith" shows what would have happened if Herbert had succumbed to his earthly desire for physical satisfactions and had abandoned his reason. By imagining man as an object, a Phantom with no conception of true Being, Coleridge can only ask unanswerable questions which all finally reduce to the single, despairing "why live?" And even that question is absurd because Coleridge's object-man has already identified himself with his Phantom world so that his desires "mean but themselves." He has, like Narcissus, already begun to experience death. Herbert's poem, by contrast, shows how desire can be educated through experience and man can import meaning into his natural existence. Because Herbert never suffered from what R. D. Laing calls "existential gangrene,"[21] he is a subject talking to another subject, and his dialogue can be completed in time. Being is not postponed. He never asks "why must we live?" only "how must we live?"

In "The Collar," poetic form mirrors self-conflict but the poet's disorderly rhymes and restive meter are the means to an end, just as Herbert's active, energetic questions portend the efficacy of prayer. The prodigal returns home and re-learns what he already knew: that in His service a man has perfect freedom. At the very end, form triumphs over existential Being, and the calm regularity of the meter belies the human belligerence signified by the diction, "rav'd" and "fierce" and "wilde":

> But as I rav'd and grew more fierce and wilde
>   At every word,
> Me thoughts I heard one calling, *Child!*
> And I reply'd, *My Lord.*

Herbert's meaning is incorporated in poetic form, or in other words, form is the meaning of Herbert's work in general. He probably would not have understood Coleridge's "fragment" of an unresolved spiritual life, or the "negative faith" which allowed him to entertain his own "unconscious unbelief." Herbert's retrospective vision is so contrary to Coleridge's generally prospective one that this contrast helps us understand Coleridge's fragments in which both meaning

[21] R. D. Laing's phrase seems appropriate for Coleridge. *The Divided Self* (London: Penguin Books Ltd., 1965. Pelican Edition), p. 133.

and final form are held in abeyance. One critic speculates that Herbert "does not begin to compose a poem until he has resolved it,"[22] and another makes the more general statement that a "picture of a spiritual conflict is written after, not during it."[23] But even though Coleridge acknowledged, as a general rule for artistic form, that "the end must be determined and understood before it can be known what the rules are or ought to be" (ShC,I,50), we must accept the possibility that the "end" for a poem might be the revelation of immediate confusion, doubt, and—the word is Coleridge's—"alienation." What the young poet called "shapings of the unregenerate mind" (PW,I,102) were Phantoms that remained with him and could not be expunged by Herbert's orthodoxy and "ceremonious" imagination.

In "Human Life" Coleridge provides a fragment of form that is appropriate for a fragmented man, not one who has rebelled against God but one who has denied Him. Alone in a Phantom world, the man hears no opposing voice to name him, only a "blank" nature that can originate "nothing." With reason separated from understanding, and meaning separated from form, Coleridge's man lacks the power to respond to his relentless inquisitor. The poet is, of course, both parties: he articulates despair but can picture it only as an "eddy without progression." The two imperfect Shakespearean sonnets that constitute "Human Life" lack any logical movement toward a positive conclusion. Accepting the absurd premise with which Coleridge begins, the speaker, by means of disorderly transitions, departs on a journey that turns back on itself. The sonnet form resembles a cage in which man restlessly searches for his "meaning," or a "drone-hive strange of phantom purposes," with drone suggesting both a monotonous sound and the male bee that

[22] Helen Vendler, *The Poetry of George Herbert* (Cambridge, Mass.: Harvard University Press, 1975), p. 132.

[23] Rosemond Tuve, quoted in Vendler's *Poetry of George Herbert*, p. 233.

has no sting and gathers no honey—a condition Coleridge ascribed to himself in "Work without Hope." The rhyme scheme of the opening sonnet is strictly Shakespearean for the first two quatrains, but the third deviates from this scheme (efee) and the final couplet continues the dropped rhyme (ff). Lacking either logical or psychological development, the form of this poem seems to be breaking down from the inside, as a vain energy ("surplus") overflows the lineaments of a conventional artistic form. Perhaps Coleridge is saying that the form cannot have perfection if man does not. The final couplet provides no resolution, since no argument has been set forth. The forms of both man and sonnet are "nigh-finished," lacking formal integrity, and it is appropriate that the rhyme scheme breaks down just as the image of the incomplete vase appears. The couplet identifies man and nature (nature made, not nature making) and the only past tense in the poem occurs here: nature "formed" man, hence he is an unconscious object, deprived of Being.

In the second sonnet, the rhyme scheme changes and the poet recharges his negative outlook through the deadly "If." But again the poem proceeds in a random way, impelled forward by questions and assertions that merely accumulate details, making a "form" by accretion. Despite the more uniform rhymes (abba/cddc/effe), the quatrains do not hold together as units, but the poem does intensify, seeming to find a direction of movement, as the assertions become more abusive. The final couplet, which would have satisfied one superficial requirement of a sonnet, is followed by an additional line that thwarts conventional expectation.[24] As if pounding in the last coffin nail, Coleridge seals the fate of man—not everyman, only man when he is with-

---

[24] Coleridge could easily have corrected his faulty rhyme by dropping the extra line. The poem was perhaps called a "fragment" in order to resist the "emptiness" and "unreality" that accompanies a "given form" (BL,II,257).

out consciousness of Being. Coleridge's experience of chaos is radically different from Herbert's "formalized picture of chaos."[25]

Both of the sonnets that make up "Human Life" show what is happening now to every sick soul who is trapped in Phantom nature and alienated from Being. Although he praised Herbert for both his Christian piety and his poetic art, Coleridge knew that he could not fit his own private anguish comfortably within Herbert's conventional form. In speaking of prayer, Coleridge distinguished three kinds: public, family, and private or solitary. He wrote that Herbert joined those who "in their dread of enthusiasm, will-worship, insubordination, indecency, carried their preference of the established public forms of prayer almost to superstition by exclusively both using and requiring them even on their own sickbeds" (LR,III,224). As "Idoloclastes Satyrane," Coleridge felt compelled to shatter the public forms Herbert found satisfying. Only then could his individual and solitary self emerge and begin its evolution toward ultimate Being. Like physical nature, fixed poetic form was a Phantom that could lure one "almost to superstition." In "Human Life" Coleridge presents a fragmented life and confronts a present and private dread, with no certainty of escape. Accepting God's orderly creation, George Herbert could not, as Joseph Summers says, "present himself, publicly at least, in disorder before God."[26] Like Aaron, Herbert comes before his readers "well-dressed." But as time has brought new forms for the Christian life, Coleridge's disheveled holiness becomes more understandable.

[25] Joseph H. Summers, *George Herbert: His Religion and Art* (Cambridge, Mass.: Harvard University Press, 1954), pp. 90-92.
[26] Summers, *George Herbert: His Religion and Art*, p. 74.

"On the threshold of some Joy, that cannot be entered into while I am embodied."
(CN,III,3370)

# 3. Limbo

Coleridge believed that "true being is not contemplatable in the forms of time and space" (LR,III,320), and yet as a poet he was compelled to find images for his earthly existence from which true Being could emerge. To represent his life accurately, he had to mingle the true and the false, the world he lived in and the one he imagined for himself. His Being was sometimes "blind and stagnant" and sometimes illuminated by a renewing light from within. More often, however, it could be found in a transitional state, and the ultimate metaphor for this condition occurs in his sublime poem "Limbo" in which time and space are being transcended. But before we consider this extraordinary work, we might look at a lesser poem that Coleridge was composing perhaps during the same period of time. It is one in which the poet attempts to create a clear allegory for two "states" of Being, here represented by a sister and a brother who are running a race. The title alone, "Time, Real and Imaginary," indicates that the contemplative poet is confronting a situation in which "extremes meet," and his conjunction acts as a sign directing us to look beyond the seeming nostalgia and sentimentality of the subject matter toward its metaphoric significance.

Time, Real and Imaginary
An Allegory

On the wide level of a mountain's head,
(I knew not where, but 'twas some faery place)
Their pinions, ostrich-like, for sails out-spread,
Two lovely children run an endless race,
    A sister and a brother!

This far outstripp'd the other;
Yet ever runs she with reverted face,
And looks and listens for the boy behind:
For he, alas! is blind!
O'er rough and smooth with even step he passed,
And knows not whether he be first or last.

(PW,I,419-420)

In an earlier version of "Time, Real and Imaginary," Coleridge's allegory is explicit: "a sort of Emblem 'Tis of Hope and Time." Hope is represented by the sister who runs ahead looking backward; Time is the blind brother who runs but cannot realize any direction.[1] By the time the poet came to revise the poem for *Sibylline Leaves*, he probably realized that Hope should look forward, not backward, and that in spite of blindness one can have direction and strive toward ultimate Being. Coleridge added a note: "by imaginary Time, I meant the state of a school boy's mind when on his return to school he projects his being in his day dreams, and lives in his next holidays, six months hence; and this is contrasted with real Time" (PW,I,419). The poet may have undergone an actual experience that years later he was trying to give a meaning to.[2] He never found allegory a congenial mode because it required a "disjunction of Faculty,"[3] but by relating the boy and girl to a single idea he could contemplate his own paradoxical attitude toward time. Coleridge would have agreed with Eliot that "to be conscious is not to be in time," but also that "only

[1] See George Whalley, *Coleridge and Sara Hutchinson and the Asra Poems* (London: Routledge & Kegan Paul, 1955), pp. 17-18.

[2] "These lines may embody some school-boy dream of holidays and his sister Ann; it may even have received some shape in boyhood, but not its present shape—that must have been impressed at a later date, probably c. 1815-17, when *Sib. Leaves* was in the press" (James Dykes Campbell, *The Poetical Works of Samuel Taylor Coleridge* [London: Macmillan, 1893], p. 638). See also CN,III, 4048n.

[3] "The advantage of symbolical writing over allegory, that it presumes no disjunction of Faculty—simple *predomination*" (CN,III,4503).

through time is time conquered." The poet's imagination must be Janus-faced, capable of looking backward and forward in order to avoid being trapped in an isolated present. The poet dislocates himself and his reader by creating some "faery place," some Limbo, where races are never won because they are endless, but where, blind to time and space and possessed of inward light, we may move freely, independent of the natural world.

The notebook entry relating to "Time, Real and Imaginary" seems a necessary part of the poem since it amplifies, through other images, the ideas implicit in the poet's "sort of emblem." Having failed to clarify his meaning by means of explicit allegory, Coleridge attempts a straightforward commentary on the poem that "ought to be":

> Contrast of troubled manhood, and joyously-active youth, in the sense of Time. To the former Time, like the Sun in a empty Sky is never seen to move, but only to *have moved*—there, there it was—& now tis here— now distant—yet all a blank between/ To the latter it is as the full moon in a fine breezy October night— driving on amid Clouds of all shapes & hues & kindling shifting colors, like an Ostrich in its speed—& yet seems not to have moved at all—This I feel to be a just image of time real & time as felt, in two different states of Being—The Title of the Poem therefore (for Poem it ought to be) should be Time real, and Time felt (in the sense of Time) in Active Youth/ or Activity and Hope & fullness of aim in any period/ and in despondent objectless Manhood—Time *objective* & subjective. (CN,III,4048)

But Coleridge's later gloss, like the gloss for *The Ancient Mariner*, tends to add or develop meaning; it provides further material for the reader's imagination to work on. As in other instances, one can perhaps question which language is more effective: the routine simile of the poem ("Their pinions, Ostrich-like") or the prose ("like an Ostrich in its speed"). The latter seems more powerfully to evoke some "unity of being," the image merging with its validating power, that Coleridge often indicates with the preposition "in." Since Coleridge's own divided self is the ultimate subject of his poem, no single illustrative metaphor could represent his "reality," and hence his poem, like ideal Being itself, provides only a possibility of unity. Metaphor is his means of seeking and approaching reality, but "the understanding of Metaphor for Reality . . . covers the world with miscreations & reptile monsters" (CN,II,2711). Both poem and explanation disclose a life of unresolved oppositions, an "endless race." Neither the brother nor his sister could alone represent Being, since Being for Coleridge quickens in the nexus of his two states of mind.

Coleridge's "two states of Being" seem essential to each other; they depend on one another for definition. The poet claimed to have loved Sara Hutchinson "in prospect, in retrospect" (CN,III,3303), but what he often endured was the "negative Being" resulting from a *present* in which he enjoyed no love object: "despondent objectless manhood." In this troubled state—a condition found in many poems, most notably "Dejection: An Ode"—he remains passive, his outer world a blank. The sister figure suggests *natura naturata*; her retrospective vision can only comprehend things made, not things in the making. By only looking backward, potential power from within is thwarted and life becomes a series of completed but discontinuous moments. With her face reverted, the girl seems to be trapped by the phantoms of time and space, by appearances, and by her own physical senses: she "looks" and "listens" for what is past. Unlike her brother who follows, she is limited, for, as Coleridge wrote, "whatever is presented to our senses (to the *outward* senses in Space, and to the *inner* sense in Time) is contemplated and apprehended, as it *appears* to us, not as it is in itself."[4] If she is supposed to embody "Time real," she represents a partial conception of reality, despite

[4] Alice D. Snyder, *Coleridge on Logic and Learning* (New Haven: Yale University Press, 1929), p. 99.

her human sympathy for her brother. She seems to lack a guiding "idea" of Hope that evidently provides her brother with his goal, even when that goal cannot be verified by the senses. Her feeling may be like one that Coleridge described for himself: "one blank Feeling, one blank idealess Feeling" (CL,II,991).

The other state of Being, embodied in the blind boy, we might call existential Being. The boy's "joyously active youth" allies him with *natura naturans*: he resembles the ever-seeking poet who uses his imagination to create a "reality" that the backward-looking understanding cannot conceive of. His goal, because it is not situated in time and space, allows him the freedom to be and the strength to disregard what Coleridge called the "clockwork" of the eighteenth century. By identifying the blind boy with creating nature, Coleridge is able to turn his abstraction of time into a metaphor, even a symbol, whereby he can affirm his own potential for self-realization. As he wrote, time is a symbol of "the Self-affirmance as the Unity" and space is a symbol of "the Self-affirmedness as the Omneity" (CL,IV, 768). What the youth "knows not" may be simply the "blank" phenomenal world, and he needs no signposts to tell him that "the stream of time [is] continuous as Life and a symbol of Eternity, inasmuch as the Past and the Future are virtually contained in the Present" (LS,29). In his commentary on "Time, Real and Imaginary," the poet unites his blind boy with an energized nature. As is common in Coleridge, participles indicate the motion that the poet felt was a synthesis of time and space, and without which time and space are "mere *abstractions*" (CL,IV,775). The positive state of Being is always active: the moon is *driving* on, *kindling shifting* colors. Only to a Phantom understanding does it "seem" not to move. Coleridge may be ,ironically suggesting that it is the girl who joins those people for whom Being is "an alien of which they know not . . . the very words that convey it are as sounds in an unknown language, or as the vision of heaven and earth expanded by the rising sun, which falls but as warmth on the eye-lids of the blind" (*Friend*,1,515). The boy, despite his blindness, or perhaps because of it, moves without apparent difficulty, and his impulsive action may suggest that he possesses "Hope" and thus "fullness of aim in any period." Although the boy "knows not" the ways of the world, he acts *as if* he knows, just as the poet through his *as if* strives for an experience beyond the reaches of the understanding: "I know not where." Being is in the world, but not of it. Thus, years later in "The Improvisatore," Coleridge as the "Sage of Highgate" tells his young listeners to cultivate a mind that:

> While it feels the beautiful and the excellent in the beloved as its own, and by right of love appropriates it, can call Goodness its Playfellow; and dares make sport of time and infirmity, while, in the person of a thousand-foldly endeared partner, we feel for aged Virtue the caressing fondness that belongs to the Innocence of childhood, and repeat the same attentions and tender courtesies which had been dictated by the same affection to the same object when attired in feminine loveliness or in manly beauty. (PW,1,465)

The pursuit of an actual object (a person existing in space and time) must be replaced by that of an ideal object, "virtue," that is emphatically *in* the person. Agape has replaced Eros. One can "make sport of time and infirmity" only when one is moving beyond them.

Coleridge wishes to merge thought and Being, but like Kierkegaard after him, he realizes that he must exist in time, with only "the process of becoming." Time real and time imaginary, like thought and feeling, or motive and impulse, should be one, but such unity was beyond the reach of the poet's metaphors. In order to rationalize his loss of youth and innocence, Coleridge had ended the first version of "Youth and Age" by declaring:

> Life is but thought: so think I will
> That Youth and I are house-mates still.

But the poet could not "will" this Phantom reasoning permanently; almost a decade later he returns to his poem and defines his temporal existence as a sad process of "tedious taking-leave" (PW,I,440). Likewise, "Time, Real and Imaginary" is unable successfully to reduce human life to ideas about life. The poet cannot choose between his "two different states of Being" without denying one part of himself, one aspect of reality; for "negative reality" was also *felt*, and by Coleridge, powerfully felt. The brother and the sister are both in motion, indicating again that Coleridge's personal Being arises from the dynamic relationship between opposites. Not only are the tenses of his poem mingled (it *was* a place where the children *run*), but, the poet's ambiguous use of "sense" suggests some ultimate definition that includes both what we know through sense perception and what we know through inner feeling, the blind boy's feeling that escapes "that Slavery of the Mind to the Eye and the visual Imagination or fancy under the influence of which the Reasoner must have a *picture* and mistakes surface for substance" (PL,434). In his objective thinking, Coleridge could assert the "power of Feelings over Images" (CN,II, 2600), but in the subjective "faery place" of "Time, Real and Imaginary" the poet constructs Being from both the natural image and from that for which the image stands. Coleridge's struggle with words as things and words as thoughts could not be ended by a choice between opposites, but by an act in time that is not bound by time:

> And like a flower that coils forth from a ruin,
> I feel and seek the light I can not see!
>
> (PW,II,912, II.324-25)

The power that "coils forth" from nature does so also in man: we have the capability of feeling and seeking. But the poet caught between two states of Being, with a language that both presents and represents, must endure contradiction in order to point toward a divine reason that is "aloof from time and space" (ShC,I,198). He believed that all "Ideas" concerning eternity could only be expressed, because of our limited understanding, through "two contradictory positions." And he distinguished eternity in the "negative sense as the mere absence of succession," from eternity as God (LR,IV,394).

୫୫୫

AROUND the same time that he was struggling with the allegory of "Time, Real and Imaginary," Coleridge was creating what he later recognized as "some of the most forcible lines" and "the most original Imagery" that he had ever achieved. In "Limbo" (PW,I,429-31;CN,III,4073-74) the poet dispenses with allegory, with the "Similitudes or Allegories" that he found so offensive in Henry Moore's poems (CN,III,4316), and creates a purely symbolic work, one whose relationship of images is made meaningful through "passion, or universal logic" and not through "the logic of grammar" (MC,163-64). Coleridge's "Limbo" is in the tradition of the religious sublime, but that tradition, like the Roman Catholic dogma that serves as the poem's *donné*, is an inherited public form that had to be violated so that the poet's Being could shine through. Limbo is one of the poet's grandest metaphors of Being, and it ultimately has little to do with the Catholic "notions," as he called them, of Limbo and Purgatory. Coleridge compared the mind to a kaleidoscope that can bring symmetry to various shapes provided by the past. The form or pattern is produced by the kaleidoscope, not by the fragmentary materials it contains. "And be assured that the time will come," he prophesies, "when the particular knowledges themselves taken separately from the form, in which the mind arranges them . . . will appear to you of not much greater comparative Value, than the fragments of glass" (CL,VI,635; also AR,258).

If Coleridge could believe that the pious Anglican George Herbert could bring "the established public forms of prayer almost to superstition" (LR,III,224), his antipathy toward Roman Catholic doctrines was a certainty.[5] In his letters and notebooks, the poet missed few opportunities of criticizing "Purgatory, Popery, the Inquisition, and other monstrous abuses" (CIS,51). And chiefly because he dreaded idols of sense, or "picture language," he was always alert to "the evil consequences of introducing the *idolon* of time as an *ens reale* into spiritual doctrines, thus understanding literally what St. Paul had expressed by figure and adaptation. Hence the doctrine of a middle state, and hence Purgatory with all its abominations" (LR,III,92).[6] Compelled to use physical images, Phantom "ends" of nature and dogma, the poet must transform them into a vehicle for revealing his own inner Being. Coleridge's rejection of dogmatic religious thought was but an extension of his opposition to predetermined or mechanical form in poetry, attesting once again to his essential coherence of thought and belief. Limbo and Purgatory for Coleridge were what pre-existence was for Wordsworth in his "Intimations Ode": a "knowledge" to be cast aside once the poet's "form" had arranged it. They were thoughts to be entertained, and they could be entertaining, as in this playful epitaph Coleridge created, in his final year, for Thomas Fuller:

A Lutheran Stout, I hold for Goose-and-Gaundry
Both the Pope's Limbo and his fiery Laundry:
No wit e'er saw I in Original Sin,

[5] Coleridge believed that Herbert's admirers must have a "constitutional predisposition to Ceremoniousness" (MC,244). Although Coleridge could write, "I find more substantial comfort, now, in pious George Herbert's 'Temple' . . . than in all the poetry, since the poems of Milton" (CL,IV,893), he nevertheless rejected Herbert's self-sufficient form.

[6] For some qualification of my interpretation of Coleridge's view of the doctrine of Purgatory see J. Robert Barth, *Coleridge and Christian Doctrine* (Cambridge, Mass.: Harvard University Press, 1969), p. 194.

And no Sin find I in Original Wit;
But if I'm all in the wrong, and, Grin for Grin,
Scorch'd Souls must pay for each too lucky hit,—
Oh, Fuller! much I fear, so vast thy debt,
Thou art not out of Purgatory yet;
Tho' one, eight, three and three this year is reckon'd,
And thou, I think, didst die *sub* Charles the Second.

(PW,II,975)

What Coleridge feared about Catholicism was that its "confining form" could stifle his "free life." For him, life and form were "two conflicting principles" (BL,II,235) out of which Being could arise, but clearly the conflict could never be resolved by any earthly authority outside of the self, especially if this authority was fixed within a social institution called Roman Catholicism. In another instance where he speaks of poetry, Coleridge could have been discussing religion: "could a rule be given from *without*, poetry would cease to be poetry, and sink into a mechanical art" (BL,II,65). The individual poet or scholar must assert Being against the pressures of conformity, as Coleridge dramatically demonstrates in lines he wrote "Suggested by the Last Words of Berengarius" (PW,I, 460-61). Like Coleridge, the rationalist scholar Berengarius of Tours (ca. 1000-1088) was a free thinker, but in a darker age of enforced conformity. He was condemned by the church fathers because he considered the Eucharist to be merely a sign or symbol, and not the transubstantiated body and blood of Christ. Like Coleridge, he apparently feared the identification of spirit with matter, and accepted the human consciousness as the appropriate realm for spiritual acts. In his poem, Coleridge condemns the clergy not because they differed with Berengarius on doctrine, but because they engaged in "learned strife" rather than in the struggle for Being. The clergy move in darkness, as do the moles in "Limbo," trapped in time, antagonistic toward that inner light which would cure their blindness. Both the poet and the religious thinker remain solitary by necessity, refusing to be confined by history or religious orthodoxy. Time does not free us from the struggle for Being, nor does history give us a clearer perspective on this struggle, since we learn from the past only what we want to learn.

Yet despite his ridicule of "the doctrine of a middle state" and other Catholic "notions," Coleridge had lived most of his life on that border where Phantom and fact meet, and he needed no theological contrivance to speak for him. His "rash imagination," as he called his creative faculty in lines he later added to "Limbo," was continually leading him into a realm that George Herbert never explored in his poetry, a realm where doubt and uncertainty could not be overpowered by an established order expressed in an assertion of belief at the poem's end. In "Limbo" Coleridge enters the poet's reverie, different from either dreaming or waking consciousness, and revitalizes an old metaphor for his two states of Being that are not to be unified in time and space. The surface fragmentation of "Limbo" is essential in order for the poet to point toward his ulterior Being, and like Shakespeare before him, Coleridge had to use paradox in order to release meaning. As Shakespeare does in *King Lear*, Coleridge employs paradox not as a fallacious mingling of two kinds of sight, nor as contradiction, but as a way of restoring us to the human experience that we must continually reassess and re-evaluate. By reconsidering our language, we reconsider ourselves. Both poets knew that physical blindness could precede another kind of seeing, and the fact that Coleridge later wished "Limbo" to be heard as the mad utterance of a poet in Bedlam (CL,VI,758,779) further suggests a kinship with Shakespeare's method.

Coleridge uses the sight-blindness paradox of "Limbo" and its companion poem "Ne Plus Ultra" as a means of escaping from the Understanding's Phantom logic and from a kind of descriptive poetry that could only copy nature's appearances, in themselves false and delusive. The lines written earlier, called "Moles," discuss overtly those materialists for whom the "unsubstantial shows of existence . . . are but *negations* of sight" (*Friend*,I,512). Trapped in the created rather than the creating world, they listen for the light they cannot see, but because they are not "possessed with inward light," as are the blind Homer in Coleridge's "Fancy in Nubibus" (PW,I,435) and the scholar Berengarius, a "Lynx amid moles," (PW,I,461), they dread the external power that defines their prison. Physical nature is accessible to the physical sight, but if all that we can see is *nature* then we are like Rousseau, "shy of light as the mole" (*Friend*,I,132). Neither cultural primitivism nor a narcissistic self that finds its reflection in nature was acceptable to Coleridge. Moreover, to confuse God with His creation was an error that he suspected even in his revered Wordsworth (CL,v,95). True Being appears when God's light, shining in and through nature, marries the light that comes from within man. Such a rare Unity of Being is what Coleridge had imagined for his beloved Sara, as we saw in the poem "Phantom": "She, she herself, and only she,/ Shone through her body visibly." At one with God and Nature, man possesses integrated vision. In the words of St. Matthew: "the light of the body is the eye: if therefore thine eye be single, thy whole body shall be full of light." But in "Limbo" man's Being is divided; the speaker is alienated from man, nature, and God, but he intensely feels his need for all three.

Coleridge began to use blindness as a metaphor for both spiritual deprivation and potential spiritual fulfillment as early as 1799, when he wrote to a friend: "I have, at times, experienced such an extinction of *Light* in my mind, I have been so forsaken by all the *forms* and *colourings* of *Existence*, as if the *organs* of Life had been dried up; as if only simple *Being* remained, blind and stagnant!" (CL,I,470). This "simple Being" was, in other words, the blindness of "negative Being," and it appears in numerous poems and notebook entries. It stands in marked contrast with the poet's positive use of blindness in a very late letter concerning the death of a friend: "in Christ only did he build a

94

# Limbo (the complete notebook entry)

*f145*  4073 18.286 *Crathmocraulo's* Thoughts like Lice—They don't *run* in his Head, as in other men's; but he scratches it— that wakens them—& then they begin to *crawl*—and this increases his *Itching* (to be witty) & so he scratches it again.— At most, his Lice & his Sense, which I suppose is what he means by his "poetic Licence", differ only as the note of a Cat & a Hawk—the one *mews*, & the other *pews*—the L~~ouse~~ice crawls & the Thoughts drawl.—Hence when he murders some dull Jest which he has caught from some other man, he aptly calls it cracking a Joke—His ⟨own are too sluggish, even to change their Quarters—⟩ Tungstic Acid's ~~Thoug~~ Wit is of the Flea kind—skips & bites—& his Jokes Flea-skips & Flea-bites— but they leave a mark behind them, much of the same depth & duration—

Copioso deems his genius mercurial—and truly it *is* very like a Salivation—it flows from him without effort; but it is but Dribble after all—

(As when the Tempest *scours* the Heaven bright.)          *f145ᵛ*
~~See Crathmocraulo, hear Tungstic quip and quibble~~
~~And~~ Huge Tungtubig has such a *hungry* Wit
That his Mouth waters at a lucky Hit.
But the Stream~~s~~ pass~~es~~ing o'er a poison'd ground,
~~And~~ The poor ⟨dead⟩ Jests, like Gudgeons drugg'd and drown'd,
Float, wrong side up, in a full Flow of Dribble:
⟨While Crawl, *whose earth-worm Wit* lives under ground,
Slow wriggles up to Light in some laborious Quibble—⟩


On Donne's first Poem.
Be proud, as Spani~~s~~hards! and ~~Skip~~ Leap for Pride, ye Fleas
Henceforth in Nature's *Minim* World Grandees,
In Phœbus' Archives registered ~~I see~~ are ye—
~~Your Letters~~ And this your Patent of Nobility.
No Skip-Jacks now, nor civiller Skip-Johns~~,~~
~~But Saintly~~
~~I hail you one and all~~
Dread Anthropophagi! Specks of living Bronze,
I hail you one & all, sans Pros ~~an~~ or Cons,
Descendants from a noble Race of *Dons*.

What tho' that great ancestral Flea be gone
Immortal with immortalizing Donne—
His earthly Spots ~~clean'd~~ ⟨burnt out⟩ bleach'd off as
~~Ghostmen~~ Papists gloze,
In purgatory fire on Bardolph's Nose,
Or else starved out, his aery tread defied
By the dry Potticary's ~~parchment~~ bladdery Hide,
Which cross'd unchang'd and still keeps in ghost-Light
Of lank Half-nothings his, the thinnest Sprite

*f146*    The sole true ~~Any~~ *Something* this in Limbo Den
It frightens Ghosts as Ghosts here frighten men—
Thence cross'd unraz'd and shall, ~~at~~ some ~~dire~~ fated Hour,
Be pulverized by Demogorgon's Power
And given as poison, to annilate Souls—
~~Even now it~~ Even now it shrinks them! ~~inwards! and~~
    they shrink in, as Moles
(Nature's mute Monks, live Mandrakes of the ground)
Creep back from Light, then listen for its Sound—
See but to dread, and dread they know not why
The natural Alien of their negative Eye

---

~~Tis a strange Place, this Limbo! for not a Place~~
~~We will never call it~~ Yet name it so/where Space &
    Time, lank Space
And scythe~~less~~ Time with jointless branny Hands
Barren and soundless as the meas'ring Sands
Mark'd but by Flit of Shades/unmeaning they
As moon-light on the Dial of the Day

---

Tis a strange Place, this Limbo! not a Place,
Yet name it ~~that~~ so—where Time & ~~hungry~~ weary Space
Fetter'd from flight, with night-mair sense of Fleeing
Strive for their last crepuscular Half-being—
Lank Space, and ⟨scytheless⟩ Time with ~~scytheless~~ branny
    Hands
Barren and soundless as the measuring Sands,

*f146ᵛ*    Mark'd but by Flit of Shades—unmeaning they
As Moonlight on the Dial of the Day—
But that is lovely—looks like Human Time,
An old Man with a steady Look sublime
That stops his earthly Task to watch the Skies—

96

But he is blind—a statue hath such Eyes—
Yet having moon-ward turn'd his face by chance—
Gazes the orb with moon-like Countenance
With scant ~~grey~~ white hairs, with fore-top bald & high
He gazes still, his eyeless Face all Eye—
As twere an Organ full of silent Sight
His whole Face seemeth to rejoice in Light/
Lip touching Lip, ~~with~~ all moveless, Bust and Limb,
He seems to gaze at that which seems to gaze on Him!

No such sweet Sights doth Limbo Den immure,
Wall'd round and made a Spirit-~~goa~~jail secure
By the mere Horror of blank Nought at all—
Whose circumambience doth these Ghosts enthrall.
A lurid Thought is growthless dull ~~Nega~~Privation,
But the Hag, Madness, scalds the Fiends of Hell
With frenzy-dreams, all incompassible
Of aye-unepithetable ~~Priv~~ Negation                    *f147*

For ~~Fate or Guile prevail'd~~ skimming in the wake, it    *f149*
    mock'd the care
Of the Old Boat-God for his Farthing Fare,
Tho' Irus' Ghost itself he neer ⟨frown'd⟩ blacker on,
The skin and skin-pent ~~Doctor~~ Druggist crost the
    Acheron,
Styx and with Puriphlegethon Coÿcytus:
The very names, methinks, might thither fright us—
Unchang'd it cross'd & shall &c

A lurid thought is growthless dull ~~Negation~~ Privation
Yet that is but a Purgatory Curse
Hell knows a fear far worse,
A fear, a future fate. Tis *positive* ~~Privation~~ Negation!

A Specimen of the Sublime dashed to pieces by cutting too
close with her fiery Four in Hand round the corner of Nonsense—

4074  18.287
        Sole Positive of Night!                              *f147*
            Antipathist of Light!

97

Fate's only Essence! Primal Scorpion Rod!
　The one permitted Opposite of God!
　　Condensed Blackness, and Abysmal Storm
　　　Compacted to one Sceptre
　　　　Arms thye Grasp enorm,
　　　　　~~Here~~ The Intercepter!
The Substance, that still casts the Shadow, Death!
　　　The Dragon foul and fell!
　　　　The unrevealable
　　　And hidden one, whose Breath
Gives Wind and Fuel to the fires of Hell!
　　　　Ah sole Despair
　　　Of both th' Eternities in Heaven!
　　Sole Interdict of all-bedewing Prayer,
　　　　The All-compassionate!
　　　Save to the Lampads seven
Revealed to none of all th' Angelic State,
　　　Save to the Lampads seven
　　　That watch the Throne of Heaven!

hope—yea, he blessed the emptiness, that made him capable of his Lord's Fullness, gloried in the Blindness that was receptive of his Master's Light" (CL,VI,922). Coleridge's "negative capability"—and we must use the term that Keats denied him—enabled the poet to conceive of a composite "form" called "Limbo," a metaphor that could encompass both blindness as ignorance and blindness as a willed means of finding God. The blind old man in Coleridge's poem is no serene image of assured sainthood, no embodiment of pure faith, because Coleridge does not allow himself God-like omniscience. The line "He seems to gaze at that which seems to gaze on him!" is accepting of man's inability to know spiritual truth with certainty. The poet's "seeming" likewise acknowledges the limitations of poetic language, as in Milton's line on Death: "what seem'd his head/ The likeness of a Kingly Crown had on" (PL,II,672-73).

Coleridge never, however, claimed to justify God's ways; he only suffered them. He recognized his own inadequacy: he is that "half-nothing" and yet "something," a body moving toward decay and a soul struggling to find God, within the "ghost light" of Limbo. The poet knew that the imagination could seize an arbitrary control over time and space, whereas "the reason is aloof from time and space" (ShC,I, 198). Being neither pure reason nor debased understanding, the imagination was capable of finding a shape to express his personal *feeling* of alienation. The imagination could embrace opposing states of Being, even if it could not perfectly marry them. Coleridge's divided self is exemplified by the moles shrinking from the light and the old man welcoming it, by both "growthless" thought and the creative light. Conflicts that the poet could sometimes resolve intellectually in his prose writings remained to be dealt with in that zone where logical argument (with its beginning, middle and end) loses its force, and where two opposites can be equally true. Coleridge came to believe that his son Hartley, the free spirit capable of integrated Being, the "one life," had come to a bad end as a result of his "shrinking from all

things connected with painful associations" (CL,v,119). But
the poet knew that his son's weakness was also his own:
guilt remained even when the mind indicated that there was
no *cause* for guilt. He wrote in 1820: "[I] shrink from all
occasions that threaten to force my thoughts back on *myself*
personally" (CL,v,126), and his fear resembles that of the
shrinking Moles who "see but to dread, and dread they
know not why." Unlike his son, Coleridge possessed a
relentless imagination that compelled him to bring his fears
to light and to face them through what he called "visual
outness." Only his words could pull unnamed fears up to
the level of consciousness and consequently free him from
"that lifeless, twilight, realm of thought, which is the confine, the *intermundium*, as it were, of existence and non-
existence" (LR,I,331). Like the Mariner's killing of the
Albatross, Coleridge's act of creating "Limbo" is perhaps
best explained as an impulse rather than a motive, and may
resemble the experience described in a notebook entry of
1812, the period of the poem:

> One of the strangest and most painful Peculiarities of
> my Nature (unless others have the same, & like me,
> hide it from the same inexplicable feeling of causeless
> shame & sense of a sort of guilt, joined with the appre-
> hension of being feared and shrunk from as a some-
> thing transnatural) I will here record—and my Motive
> or rather Impulse to do this, seems to myself an effort
> to eloign and abalienate it from the dark Adyt of my
> own Being by a *visual* Outness—& not the wish for oth-
> ers to see it—. (CN,III,4166)

T. S. Eliot once implied that George Herbert lacked the
"general awareness" of a great religious poet because he
presents us with a concluded belief: "this general awareness
may have existed; but the preliminary steps which represent it have been repressed, and only the end-product is
presented."[7] I believe that Coleridge's "Limbo" reveals such

[7] T. S. Eliot, *Essays, Ancient and Modern* (London: Faber &
Faber, 1936), p. 97.

"general awareness" and, like many of Eliot's own fragments, refuses to surrender its life and become an "end-product."

The subterranean moles, by simple synecdoche, could stand for all materialists who hide from that distant "light still struggling through a cloud," trapped in their surroundings and incapable of evolving Being. Their "negative" eyes indicate their "negative Being." Coleridge had made a direct attack on materialism from his early years onward. For example, in "Allegoric Vision" (1795), he pictures a "string of blind men, the last of whom caught hold of the skirt of the one before him, he of the next, and so on till they were all out of sight." When in his dream he asks who is guiding the procession, an "old dim-eyed man" (who turns out later to be "Superstition") explains that "the string of blind men went on for ever without any beginning; for although one blind man could not move without stumbling, yet infinite blindness supplied the want of sight." Coleridge is, of course, ridiculing both materialism and the cause-and-effect logic used by men of impoverished understanding, but the dreamer's reaction is ambivalent: "I burst into laughter, which instantly turned to terror" (PW,II,1091-96). The same ambivalence exists in the full notebook version of "Limbo," which begins with lighthearted satire and ends in metaphysical terror. Coleridge described materialism as a philosophy that "fleeing from inward alarm, tries to shelter itself in outward contempt—that is at once folly and a stumbling-block to the partizans of a crass and sensual materialism, the advocates of the Nihil nisi ab extra ['Nothing if not from without']" (Friend,I,494). But even though he could ridicule blind materialists, he knew what it was like to be deprived of inner light, and he lived with a deep-seated fear that without it he would be helplessly vulnerable to that Nothingness from without.

Whereas materialism could be aptly represented by the earthly moles, Coleridge's surrogate in the poem, the old man, needed to be liberated from the restrictions of time and space, and from the material world and its images. The moles could be related to "mandrakes of the ground," but the old man had to be urged toward his ultimate Being. He resembles an abstraction ("looks like human time"), more probably "Time Imaginary" than "Time Real," but because his *telos* exists beyond the physical world, any superficial description of the man—the human being as object, not subject—threatened to distort Coleridge's metaphor of Being. The poet's paradox does not present a truth but only the grounds for a possible truth. Coleridge describes the old man as blind and bald, with a high forehead and scanty white hair; the old man's actions can be reported as he watches and turns, but his "look sublime" can be achieved only by a "Moon-like Countenance." He is nearing eternity and becoming, as it were, a Yeatsian statue. He seems almost "out of nature," motionless, a gaze fixed on the absolute. Here Coleridge was probably remembering an actual blind man he met on a walking trip, a John Gough of Kendal: "the rapidity of his touch appears fully equal to that of sight; and the accuracy greater. Good heavens! it needs only to look at him! Why his face sees all over! It is all one eye!" (LR,I,329). The man's face, "the undisturbed *ectypon* of his own soul," found its way into Coleridge's poem.

In order to achieve some ideal image, a Yeatsian symbol of permanence, Coleridge would have had to deny his own idea of organic and spiritual evolution—of becoming—and accept at least a poetic dogma, if not a religious one. The old man stops performing his earthly tasks, but nevertheless, he is not yet the statue Coleridge compares him to. Having ended his restless search for final answers, he achieves a state of Being in which physical passivity and spiritual activity are combined. His mind is independent of the phenomenal world, and his soul is like the one described in the *Biographia Literaria*: "steady and collected in its pure *Act* of inward adoration to the great I AM" (BL,II,218). The impulse that turns the old man's face toward heaven is not governed by the rational processes of his understanding but by the grace of his imagination, which has its own logic.[8] Verbal equivocation becomes necessary in order to prevent the physical image from dominating that Being of which it is only a part. Brought into association with the "half-beings" of Limbo, but not "unmeaning," as they are, the old man "gazes still." His gaze becomes a fusion of physical action and spiritual stillness, with "still" further suggesting timelessness, but the poet withholds his commitment to arrested process or absolute Being. The "half-truth" of appearance is superior to the "half-being" of materialism only because of its *potentiality*. The poet's metaphor is his means of releasing possibility while avoiding the fixity of dogma. Not knowing what they seek, the Limbo souls are deprived of both darkness and light; they exist in a "crepuscular" state, striving only for what they *were*. But the blind old man, likewise denied both light and darkness, sees what he can *be*. He embodies Coleridge's definition of reality: "the Real exists only as the *Identity* of the actual and the potential."[9] However, such an identity can only be attained through an imaginative projection, and Limbo probably remains the single most accurate metaphor for Coleridge's own poetic life, a life lived on the border between the extremes of materialism (pure image) and mysticism (pure idea). The form and meaning of Coleridge's poem can only be considered a unified whole, for Coleridge could not rest with a transcendent vision in which "extremes meet" never to divide again. In his "Dejection: An Ode" the poet evoked joy and conferred it on the absent Sara Hutchinson, leaving for himself only the consciousness of joy. In his later poem "Limbo," still seeking a pure joy, he summons it up for another surrogate in a poem; but in his sad honesty, he pro-

[8] Coleridge would agree with Eliot that "There is a logic of the imagination as well as a logic of concepts." Preface to *Anabasis* (New York: Harcourt, Brace & Co., 1949), p. 10.

[9] Marginal note in Joseph Hughes' *Believer's Prospect and Preparation*, etc. (London, 1831), B.M.C. 126 h.2 (7).

vides his projected self with only the possibility of joy: "His whole Face *seemeth* to rejoice in Light."

Coleridge did not allow himself to worship external light, whether from sun or moon, for fear of falling victim to a Phantom "idol of sense." Light could serve only as a metaphor to suggest the power that must originate within the human soul: "from the soul itself must issue forth/ A light, a glory, a fair luminous cloud" ("Dejection: An Ode"). Even though the sun does not appear directly in "Limbo" (or in "Ne Plus Ultra"), it nevertheless issues the light from which the materialist moles shrink, creates the reflected light that the old man faces, and provides the power that defines even the "antipathist of light" in hell. Coleridge could accept the "sun" as the traditional metaphor for God's power, the source of growth and self-realization, but he was ever alert to the danger of identifying God with His creation. What we see is a gift: "Man knows God only by revelation from God—as we see the Sun by his own Light—" (CN,I,209). The moon, however, as an emblem of the human imagination, could project the false light of illusion, of self-deception, and of the unreality in dreams: "there is nothing in it that can be called tangible—nothing which presents motives or shapes itself to human imperfections. Allow the light: it is moonlight and moths float about in it!" And the poet further criticized those people who ignore painful knowledge and are content to muse beside their soporific firesides: "you have warmth; this may be a stove of life, and crickets and other insects sing their inarticulate songs in it!" (PL,226). To have no motives and to be inarticulate meant, for Coleridge, to be *identified* with external nature and to lack the will toward Being. He was dissatisfied by a counterfeit power: "the light of religion is not that of the moon, light without heat; but neither is its warmth that of the stove, warmth without light. Religion is the sun, whose warmth indeed swells, and stirs, and actuates the life of nature" (*Friend*,I,105). The *life* of nature is not nature's Being, just as man's Being is not his earthly existence. But Coleridge was not a Blakean man confidently radiating sunlight in his eternal moment; he was compelled by his own doubts and his "reflective" nature to choose the moon as a metaphor for his uncompleted Being. The poet saw Christian faith as:

> A deep and inward conviction, which is as the moon to us; and like the moon with all its massy shadows and deceptive gleams, it yet lights us on our way, poor travellers as we are, and benighted pilgrims. With all its spots and changes and temporary eclipses, with all its vain halos and bedimming vapors, it yet reflects the light that *is* to rise on us, which even now is *rising*, though intercepted from our immediate view by the mountains that enclose and frown over the vale of our mortal life. (*Friend*,I,97)

Being both *is* and is *rising*.

In "Limbo," time and space are "unmeaning" because they, like the sundial, are divorced from the world that provides their limited power. The beauty of the line "As Moonlight on the Dial of the Day" is equalled by its Horatian usefulness in representing all of man's measuring devices, the tools of his ineffectual human understanding that cannot solve the mystery of Being. The sundial recalls the Ancient Mariner's "steady weathercock" that was "steeped in silentness" by the moon and was surely no guide through rough interior weather. Within the realm of Coleridge's potent, highly suggestive sun-moon imagery, the sundial becomes more than a casual image. The poet had written that "the Conscience, I say, bears the same relation to God, as an accurate Time-piece bears to the Sun" (*Friend*,I,150-51), and that to read the Bible without the proper spirit was to read a sundial by moonlight. In fact, he employed the image to illustrate a basic principle of literary criticism: "every Book worthy of being read at all must be read in and by the same Spirit, as that by which it was written. Who does not do this, reads a Dial by moonshine."[10] Both written texts and

---

[10] Marginal note in anonymous, *Eternal Punishment Proved to Be Not Suffering, but Privation* (London, 1817), xi, B.M.C. 126 g.3.

the "text" that is the world will surrender their secrets only if a creative light is brought to bear upon them. A text does not *possess* meaning, but it can *declare* meaning—just as Being can be declared by metaphor.[11] The sun's light is absent from "Limbo," except as the power that the moles acknowledge but fear to confront directly. Coleridge knew firsthand the sin of *accidie*, the refusal of joy, and his speculations were often self-revelations. He wrote: "what if the natives of the Sun should refuse to avail themselves of the Light, which had called the Worlds around them out of Death and Darkness . . . ?" (CL,VI,773). Completely in the dark, they would suffer "negative Being," unable even to imagine joy. But Coleridge's "ghosts" in "Limbo" are conscious of their alienation, and even though they are preoccupied by the possibility of total annihilation, their "horror of blank Nought-at-all" suggests their potential for realizing an allied emotion, hope, and not fear. The moonlight illuminating "Limbo" is a ghost light that, like Coleridge's own existence in time, can be endured because there is another light, "which even now is *rising*."

The contrast between the moles, who shun the light, and the old man, who welcomes it; the opposition of the sun and the moon; and the insufficiency of time and space when viewed against the background of eternity are demonstrations of Coleridge's characteristic use of polarities to help describe both man and nature. But in his quest for ultimate Being he often found language inadequate. Definitions and distinctions created by his understanding often acted as "toys" (CL,I,267) diverting him from his goal, and both Catholic doctrine and poetic metaphor were also only toys unless they were made to declare Being and not simply ex-

---

[11] Coleridge's use of "declare" is instructive. The Mariner declares the beauty of the water snakes and thereby momentarily frees himself from his alienation. The heavens may clearly declare the wonder of God, whereas Coleridge's expression of his own Being remains paradoxical, like the cloud that both "hides and declares" God's presence (CL,III,305).

istence. Language itself, a simple collection of words with fixed and objective meanings, could diminish Being. The poet feared that "in the Mystery of Redemption metaphors will be obtruded for the reality; and in the mysterious Appurtenants and Symbols of Redemption (Regeneration, Grace, the Eucharist, and Spiritual Communion) the realities will be evaporated into metaphors" (AR,294). As we have seen, Coleridge expressed sympathy for the scholar Berengarius because he questioned imposed form and sought the "truth within." Coleridge's struggle with language was a struggle to reach and express Being. His shift from "privation" to "negation" in the manuscript of "Limbo," as we shall see, reveals a poet seeking a name for his unique anguish.

In physical life Coleridge discovered a continuous process at work, that of opposites meeting in order to divide and begin moving toward another reconciliation. But this "Theory of Life" was not effective when, while writing "Limbo," the poet had to embark upon a metaphysical consideration of Being in terms of the fixed opposites of heaven and hell. Lacking Blake's supreme confidence, Coleridge could not imagine a happy marriage of the two; and in his uncertainty he could only conceive that "poles imply a null punct or point which being both is neither, and neither only because it is the Identity of Both" (CL,IV,771). Out of the "null punct" that is "Limbo" true Being may be rescued, but the poet's problem was to bring together abstraction and image, to locate in language, in time and space, the "strange place" that is "not a place." He had written of Milton's picture of Limbo: "how ill fancy assorts with imagination" (LR,III,61). Even this sublime poet could falter when he attempted to arrange images, "materials ready made from the law of association," into a purely imaginary creation. Coleridge knew that his personal religious experience could not be expressed or experienced in any form imposed from without, and language itself was such a form:

> Religion, in its widest sense, signifies the act and habit
> of reverencing THE INVISIBLE, as the highest both
> in ourselves and in nature. To this the senses and their
> immediate objects are to be made subservient, the one
> as its organs, the other as its exponents: and as such
> therefore, having on their own account no true *value*,
> because of no inherent *worth*. They are a *language*, in
> short: and taken independently of their representative
> function, from *words* they become mere empty *sounds*.
> (*Friend*,I,440)

These "empty sounds" must be transformed into what Coleridge in "Frost at Midnight" called "articulate sounds of
things to come." The images in "Limbo" become vital when
they begin the painful process of changing into abstractions;
they are not designed to please us, but to declare the difficulty of Being. Therefore, the poet's role "sometimes lies in
the rupture of association," and organic form "may be present in a disagreeable object" (BL,II,257). In "Limbo," time
and space have shed their familiar earthly images—space is
lank, time is scytheless—and yet they are only able to loiter
at the threshold of Being, reluctant to change, and striving
to preserve the identities they have outgrown. Thus like the
moles, whose "negative eye" signifies "negative Being," and
like the poet, who knows that "a lurid thought is growthless," all of the inhabitants of Coleridge's poem except the
old man are paralyzed by their fear of the unknown. In this
surrealistic creation, Coleridge acknowledges his own despair, but his thinking is neither "lurid" (ghostly) nor
"growthless." Even though he said as a young man, "I have
rather made up my mind that I am a mere *apparition*—a
naked Spirit" (CL,I,295), he finds, through poetry, that one
can discover Being in the world, *in the movement* from
negation to affirmation. His poem dramatically "signifies
the act and habit of reverencing THE INVISIBLE."

In his urge to unify opposites, Coleridge sought to elimi-
nate any distinction between time and space and to experience God as life, that is, as movement or energy. But he

recognized that because time and space are only language "terms," and consequently of "no inherent worth" in themselves, they could not be meaningfully applied to the idea of the Supreme Being. But because God can only be contemplated in separation from Him, the poet must serve his sentence in Limbo and, through paradox, point toward a higher synthesis. Unity can only be effected by means of opposites, but the opposite of Coleridge's "Limbo" is a power in man that is either residual or potential. Neither *mere* images nor finally *mere* abstractions can be "taken independently of their representative function":

> That both time and space are mere abstractions I am well aware; but I know with equal certainty that what is *expressed* by them as the *identity* of both is the highest reality, and the root of all power, the power to suffer, as well as the power to act. (TL,93)

Again, Coleridge's growth through poetry is remarkable. The "beauty-making power" that he lamented losing in "Dejection: An Ode" has been transformed into a greater power, the power of Being, beside which all poems are secondary. Coleridge's tolerance of these Limbo images of his own incomplete self demonstrates that what the poet sought was not an "objective correlative" but a "subjective correlative." He saw all "modern poetry" as "a fleeting away of external things, the mind or subject greater than the object, the reflective character predominant" (MC,164). The act of Being is not confined by time or space, unlike physical acts with their finite ends. Therefore, when poetry serves Being it too must outgrow the requirement for formal endings, and for the work of art as a completed object: "something inherently mean in action. Even the Creation of the Universe disturbs my Idea of the Almighty's greatness —would do so, but that I conceive that Thought with him Creates" (CN,I,1072). Coleridge's "Limbo" reveals a subject creating itself.

If Coleridge's heaven required the unity of time and

space, his concept of hell demanded their annihilation. He wished to share with Jeremy Taylor the belief that hell is only the "separation from God's presence," but he could not avoid formulating intellectually what he had experienced in the course of his own temporal history: the negation of power, rather than the satanic use of power for negative ends. The Godhead must enjoy what the poet's life could only suffer. Coleridge combines moral seriousness with a logician's play in his annotation to Taylor:

> Why, if hell be a State, and not a mere place, and a particular state; its meaning must in common sense be a state of the worst [sort]. If then there be a mere pœna damni—(i.e. not so blest as some others may be) this is a different state *in genere* from the pœna sensûs —ergo, not Hell—ergo rather, a 3rd State, or else Heaven. For every Angel must be in it, than whom another Angel is happier—i.e. *negatively* damned, tho' *positively* very happy.[12]

Coleridge confesses that like Taylor he is inclined to the belief that the only immortality exists in heaven, and that hell is simply privation or absence, but he goes back to the Bible and finds "so many texts against it!" Physical torment was a cruel punishment that Coleridge's tender nature could not bear to ascribe to the creator of the "one life." Eternal absence, even positive evil—but not positive torment. What the poet needed was a Blakean contrary: "now Reason and Common Sense informs us, that the mere Negation of a Thing is not the Contrary of that Thing. The contrary of Love is Hate, not Indifference."[13] Yet he could not even imagine a God capable of hatred, just as he could endure his own alienation from his wife or Southey or Wordsworth but could never actively hate them.

---

[12] Marginal note in Jeremy Taylor's *Polemical Discourses* (London, 1674), i 897. This annotation differs from the comment on Jeremy Taylor recorded in LR,III,317. My reading consequently varies from Father Barth's (*Coleridge and Christian Doctrine*, pp. 191-2).

[13] Marginal note in *Eternal Punishment*.

When Coleridge, prior to "completing" the poem "Limbo," returned to add the "future fate" of the inhabitants of Limbo—the description of hell that became the poem "Ne Plus Ultra"—he was unable to create an image more horrible than his metaphor of Limbo; all he could do was name, rather than present as a movement toward Being, his sublime subject. And, paradoxically, the poet's invective is metrically soothing. His portrayal of hell reveals no physical suffering, for the damned human souls cannot even be seen; Satan alone holds our attention, and his punishment is the greatest that this Christian poet could tolerate: the inability to pray, to articulate "sounds of things to come," or to recognize hidden vice through "visual outness." Although Satan is called a "foul dragon," Coleridge's urge is to pity the figure who, like himself in his despair, recognizes his exclusion from blessedness and, what is worse, his inability to move toward God. Always vulnerable and always compassionate, Coleridge could hardly conceive of a loveless vision of evil, "God present without manifestation of his presence" (BL,II,208). He could only assert rather than demonstrate the "positive negation" because, as he had written earlier, if the devil were all evil, "he would be nothing at all, which is a contradiction in terms . . . if, I say, the Devil exist, he must have some good Qualities" (CN,II, 2744).

The poet's struggle to define hell is evident in the manuscript of "Limbo," in which "privation" and "negation" are interchanged in order to indicate some progressive evolution, even if it is only from one degree of pain to a more intense one, or from "half-being" to the "blank Nought-at-all." The Limbo souls, deprived of God, reveal Coleridge's own divided Being: separation from his physical love object, Sara Hutchinson, is only a diminutive counterpart to his separation from God, the ultimate love object. Once more, Coleridge's poetic and spiritual evolution prove complementary. Progressing from natural imagery to self-made imagery, the poet sought ultimately to experience God without images. But like the "Interceptor" in hell, he knew that he had been singled out for punishment. By fusing the temporary state of Purgatory, a state that inflicts positive punishment, and the innocent but deprived state of Limbo, Coleridge forged a composite metaphor of Being. That he wavered between privation and negation, finally associating privation with Limbo and negation with Hell, suggests that the poet was struggling to make language express his evolving consciousness of Being.[14] His distinction between these two words indicates a problem with language rather than with experience, for Coleridge had truly endured both kinds of hell. His notebooks and letters record both privation—his severed communion with Sara, and his inability to pray to God—and the positive negation of bodily pain and nightmares. The two kinds of hell, like Limbo and Purgatory, were moving toward a common identity in Coleridge's metaphor. The verb "to be" was all he needed to connect absence (privation) and torment (positive negation).

It is the absolute finality of hell that Coleridge found difficult to imagine. Hell is the opposite of God and organic form, a place where no current runs between poles generating Being, a place where there is only a "sole positive," a "sole despair," a "sole interdict." The Aeolian harp that earlier found its correspondent breeze has become as solitary as a statement of dogma: it is fate's "only essence," the "one permitted opposite," the "one scepter," the "hidden one." For a poet who resisted concluding many of his poems, the idea of hell must have struck him with its necessarily fixed form, the "dead organic" (BL,II,257). Ironically, perhaps, the form in which Coleridge composed his evocation of hell, "Ne Plus Ultra," was the Pindaric ode, with its impersonal yet emotional tone, its irregular feet and rhymes, and its

[14] Coleridge faced in 1805 the spiritual problem that was also a problem of poetic representation: "Nihil *negativium*, quod est etiam irrepresentabile [a negative nothing, which cannot be presented to the mind]" and "nihil privativum cogitable [a private nothing, which is conceivable]" (CN,II,2502n).

heightened and *general* diction, for it was the worn-out vehicle for expressing the sublime—in the eighteenth century! As the ghost souls in "Limbo" are "wall'd round" by ultimate nothingness, Coleridge's Satan in "Ne Plus Ultra" is confined by the poet's powers of meter and rhyme. Incapable of self-discovery, the "hidden one" is defined by the light he denies. Far from being an "Ode to the Devil," as George Watson calls it, "Ne Plus Ultra" celebrates the power of poetry that can name the unnameable, and restrict its freedom of movement.

❧❧❧

COLERIDGE's struggle for Unity of Being was, as we have seen, paralleled by his struggle with language, and it was also mirrored in his quest for a poetic form that could be true to the changing, incoherent nature of Being-in-time. That form was by necessity a "fragment," since a work could be completed only by assuming that Being is located in the here and now. Poems are not perfect aesthetic objects, but notes left behind as the poet moves on to a new knowledge of Being. Yet, as Coleridge said in another context, "there is *method* in the fragments" (*Friend*,1,449), and it may be useful to consider the technical demands that Coleridge faced in writing "Limbo," as well as other of his late poems.

The poem "Limbo," like one of Michelangelo's statues emerging from the crude stone, may appear to some readers as a marvelous but miscarried work, an unsatisfying because unfinished object.[15] And the poem's publication history would support the contention that the poet simply yoked together some unrelated pieces of writing and, unable to

[15] The poet recognized a kinship with the sculptor: "there the mighty spirit still coming from within had succeeded in taming the untractable matter and in reducing external form to a symbol of the inward and imaginable beauty." Artistic forms, like natural ones, must possess inherent life: "we look at the forms after we have long satisfied all curiosity concerning the mere outline; yet still we look and look and feel that these are but symbols" (PL,193).

impose any order on them, added "Limbo" to his notorious gallery of abandoned works. The poem first appearead in *Poetical Works* (1834) as two poems, "Limbo" and "Moles," the latter having been printed separately in Coleridge's periodical, *The Friend*, in 1818. The two were combined in James Dykes Campbell's *Poetical Works* in 1893, and the editor's note reads: "two fragments—Moles and Limbo—first collected in P. W. 1834 and here united with their connecting context." Campbell, however, omitted Coleridge's preliminary lines, "On Donne's first Poem," whereas Ernest Hartley Coleridge later, in preparing the current standard text and working from the same manuscript evidence, chose to include them but to separate them from "Limbo" and place them elsewhere among "Jeux D'Esprit." (Some initial asterisks indicate the absent lines.) Only recently, with the publication of the third volume of Coleridge's notebooks do we see that a controlling idea pervades even the opening lighthearted satire: an idea that affirms the evolution of matter into spirit, while conveying the horror of matter divorced from spirit. Despite Coleridge's apparently eclectic selection of his poetic materials, "there is *method* in the fragments," and Kathleen Coburn is probably correct in believing that the poetic act appears to be a single impulsive performance. Limbo, by definition, is an inconclusive state, with its end projected beyond it into heaven or hell. Like Coleridge's nightmares, it was a state "during which the Understanding and moral Sense are awake, tho' more or less confused, and over the Terrors of which the Reason can exert no influence."[16] The human "Understanding" of the person (Coleridge or another) who tried to edit such an experience after the fact could impose a waking order, but the form would be suspect. When Coleridge in his last years claimed that he had "made numerous alterations and large additions" to "Limbo," and that he had received "a certain influx of thoughts that suggest an apt

[16] Quoted in Humphrey House, *Coleridge: The Clark Lectures* (London: Rupert Hart-Davis, 1953), p. 154.

conclusion and would make the thing a compleat Poem"
(CL,vi,779), he quotes from memory the original lines with
only slight variation. The feeling had found its form as a
fragment.

Coleridge's problem with creating endings was a result of
his need to make his theory of art correspond to his idea of
Being. Like poetry, "*Life* is a subject with an inherent
tendency to produce an object, wherein and whereby to
find itself,"[17] but it is Coleridge's *tendency* that reveals
Being, not any object, and the poetic form must somehow
be true to that tendency. To observe "Limbo" emerging
from its rather labored prose beginnings is to witness a
caterpillar developing into a butterfly, the poet's recurring
figure for organic form. Beginning with some lighthearted
commentary on the varieties of wit practiced by some of
his acquaintances, Coleridge soon finds that his feeling insists
on progressive movement: thoughts waken and begin to
crawl, although some are sluggish and remain behind; one
wit skips and bites, and another flows. Before long, the cata-
logue begins to divide like an organism, assuming the shape
of lines of poetry; rhymes begin to surface. The "flea wit"
is moving toward the satire of "On Donne's first Poem"
("The Flea"), and will subsequently enter "Limbo" as a
flea, "the thinnest Sprite," the "sole true Something" that
opens the poem as it is now printed. Likewise, the "earth-
worm wit" that "wriggles up to light" will evolve into the
moles of "Limbo." Coleridge could have been referring to
the form of "Limbo" when he wrote: "the grandest efforts
of poetry are when the imagination is called forth, not to
produce a distinct form, but a strong working of the mind,
still offering what is again rejected; the result being what the
poet wishes to impress, namely, the substitution of a sublime
feeling of the unimaginable for a mere image" (ShC,ii,138).

In "Limbo" (and I include the preliminary "On Donne's
first Poem") we find the poet making false starts, canceling
lines and words, overextending at times, rewriting—all the

[17] Owen Barfield, *What Coleridge Thought*, p. 67.

usual labors of a craftsman. Coleridge, moving onward from Donne, describes the "immortal flea" in its journey from the natural world into the supernatural Limbo, and without these lines the opening of "Limbo" as printed seems perversely obscure:

> The sole true Something—This! In Limbo's Den
> It frightens Ghosts, as here Ghosts frighten men.

Not only do the pronouns lack antecedent meaning, but they fail to suggest what Coleridge was actually troubled by: the absurdity of introducing phenomenal *things* into a spiritual realm. The power that moves within nature is allied with the power that evolves words into poems, but because "the forms exist before the substance out of which they are shaped"[18] the poet's Being can only be implied by his act of shaping his materials. Poetry does not just happen by itself; it is made to happen. As Coleridge explained to the son of his friend, James Gillman, nature brings the caterpillar into the moth, but only by reflection, reason, and discipline can man evolve into a higher state (CL,v,296-97). It is the form adapting itself that is organic, not the expendable images. The earthworm that "wriggles up to Light" evolves into the old man who naturally turns his face toward the light, for everything in the poem is progressing toward that end which cannot be contained in language. Coleridge's "Method implies a *progressive transition*" (*Friend*,I,457), so that the form of "Limbo," like that of the more recent "Prufrock," is only superficially fragmentary, and transitions are suppressed so that Being can escape the strictures of mechanical form. There is a vast difference between "disjecta membra" and "poetae," as Coleridge well understood (ShC,II,44).

When Coleridge's transitions are not suppressed, they often appear to defy logical explanation. His linkage seems deliberately disjointed, as, for example, in the key line "But

---

[18] Thomas Allsop, *Letters, Conversations and Recollections of S. T. Coleridge*, 2 vols. (London: Edward Moxon, 1836), I, 100.

that is lovely—looks like Human Time." After introducing
the flea into "Limbo" and describing the place that is not a
place, Coleridge moves to juxtapose the organic human being and the growthless state of limbo. But his phrase "that
is lovely," framed by two dashes in the manuscript, is ambiguous, perhaps because even in imagination Coleridge
could not fix himself permanently.[19] The old man stops his
"earthly" task, indicating that he is not within the confines
of Limbo, but the poet's imagination is striving to fuse the
*concept* of Limbo with his own individual *experience* of it.
His use of pronouns is instructive: the "This!" opening
the poem indicates that the Limbo experience is present and
near, but with the distance gained through imaginative
vision, Coleridge can use "that" to refer to his Being-in-
Time that in retrospect seems "lovely" and subsequently
"sweet." In customary prose discourse, the pronoun "that"
would refer to the preceding luminous line "As Moonlight
on the Dial of the Day," but perhaps the poet also intends
for it to anticipate its referential meaning. As a Christian
poet both in and out of time, Coleridge disrupts logical
sequence and creates a transitional hinge that can turn two
ways, just as the poet is in Limbo but also out of it. At the
end, he can say "Yet *that* is but a Purgatory curse," indicating the imagination's power to outgrow its own crea-
tions.

Wishing to make his poem a "progressive realization"
and not simply an "aggregation of words" (PL,290), Coleridge returns to Limbo proper after his evocation of the
old man, and moves toward a conclusion. But the couplet
form he chose for "Limbo" presented him with a problem;
this form is progressive but it lacks any inherent means of
conclusion. In the manuscript, he returns to the earlier idea
of crossing into Limbo (a redundant doubling back that

[19] Coleridge's numerous dashes (which Ernest Hartley Coleridge
treats rather indifferently, eliminating some, adding others), may
indicate that conventional punctuation was inadequate for the poet's
unconventional subject.

produces some lines that Ernest Hartley Coleridge chose to delete from his text), and finally produces a quatrain (abba) that contains the flow of his couplets:

> A lurid thought is growthless dull Privation
> Yet that is but a Purgatory Curse
> Hell knows a fear far worse,
> A fear, a future fate. Tis *positive Negation!*

The "free life" has been brought within the "confining form" of Limbo, and thus the content is mirrored in the form. The poem's conclusion, like "ultimate" Being, may not be found in the objective world. When Coleridge broke off his notebook entry with "A Specimen of the Sublime dashed to pieces by cutting too close with her fiery Four in Hand round the corner of Nonsense," he realized the extraordinary demands he had made on language and poetic form.

If, as Kathleen Coburn believes, Coleridge returned to the blank page following "Limbo" and inserted the complementary poem "Ne Plus Ultra," we are again faced with the truth of Valéry's statement that "no poem is ever finished." Coleridge's thrust toward the sublime may have been "dashed to pieces" by his lack of control in "Limbo," but control has certainly been exerted in the later "Ne Plus Ultra." Only two extremely minor changes (one letter altered; one word cut) mar an otherwise flawless performance. One can perhaps speculate that the poet's deeply personal feelings as well as his "rash imagination" were impelling the lines of "Limbo," whereas he was simply remaking an object, not himself, in "Ne Plus Ultra." The ode, with its interlocking rhymes reinforced by end-stopped, declarative phrases, may have represented the kind of superficial form that the poet had actively opposed by his "principle within, independent of everything without" (ShC,II,261). In "Limbo" there is notable activity: moles shrink, creep, listen, see; time and space are still striving; the old man turns and gazes. But such activity would be inappropriate to hell, and the formal problem of "Ne Plus Ultra" is how to deny the *organic* form that characterizes Coleridge's movement toward Being in both life and art. Hell is an utterly fixed, permanent state, the "dead organic," without even a flea, a "something" to introduce change.

Of the twenty-one lines that comprise "Ne Plus Ultra," fourteen are simple nominatives, descriptive phrases. The verbs that occur do not give vitality to the force of darkness, but rather to the all-powerful God who "permitted" the "positive of night" to exist. Thus God *compacts* and *arms* the Interceptor in a permanent present, while forbidding him communion with anything outside himself. Satan, unlike the poet who created "Limbo," does not even have the power to reveal himself, but must passively be "reveal'd" by an outside force. Only two active, present tense verbs give life to Satan, and they are ironically negated: the "substance" casts a shadow, but the verb's force is destroyed by our realization that in fact it is the light that *casts* the shadow, for all objective forms remain invisible unless illuminated. The second verb "gives" is also ironic because without God's grace Satan, the "positive of Night," can only renew his own self-generated suffering: his breath "gives Wind and Fuel to the fires of Hell!" Truly solipsistic, Satan enjoys *ne plus ultra*, nothing more beyond himself. Yet even in this final, conclusive spot, Coleridge had to create the Interceptor in his own image, the poet in the depths of negative Being, with no "outward and visible signs of the sacrament within":

> Poor shadow cast from an unsteady wish,
> Itself a substance by no other right
> But that it intercepted Reason's light.
>
> (PW,I,467)

In "Limbo" and "Ne Plus Ultra" Coleridge created a composite poem, combining the darkness of hell and, by implication, the light of heaven, and linking the two extremes with a moving image of "that tremendous Medium between Nothing and true Being, which Scripture & inmost Reason present as most, most Horrible!" (CL,IV,545). He wrote that "whether the Knowing of the Mind has its correlative in the Being of Nature, doubts may be felt. Never to have felt them, would betray an unconscious unbelief, which traced to its extreme roots will be seen grounded in a latent disbelief" (*Friend*,I,512). In his search for "true Being" Coleridge drew many metaphors from "the Being of Nature," but perhaps his most difficult struggle came when his imagination sent him beyond time and space into the medium of "Limbo." Poetry had for a short time effected a marriage with nature, but when that failed, poetry was still on hand to help him reach beyond nature. Poetic form, even poetic imagery, became subservient to a higher reality. As he wrote in a notebook: "Form is factitious *Being*, and Thinking is the Process. Imagination the Laboratory, in which Thought elaborates Essence into Existence" (CN,II, 3158).

"a bodiless Substance, an unborrow'd Self."
(CN,II,2921)

# 4. Beyond Metaphor: Coleridge's Abstract Self

In "Limbo" Coleridge imagined himself as an old man aspiring to that plenitude of Being that is not found within a fallen world. Like the poem itself, the old man is incomplete, a subject realizing itself through humility, an "idealess watching" (CL,II,1008). Coleridge defined two kinds of knowledge: empirical, gained through the Understanding, the faculty that bases its operations on sense objects; and spiritual, gained by the Reason through abstraction and self-reflection.[1] The Understanding forms classes and makes generalizations, but the Reason can do more: it can dissolve the presumed identity of subject and object (man and his world) and recreate a new identity on a higher level of consciousness. The first stage of this abstract reasoning, of course, is to recognize that the "Phænomenon Self is a Shadow" (CN,II,3026), and then to proceed through continual acts of will to evolve an "abstract self." Coleridge was singularly equipped (perhaps fated) to handle abstraction: "for from my very childhood I have been accustomed to *abstract* and as it were unrealize whatever of more than common interest my eyes dwelt on; and then by a sort of transfusion and transmission of my consciousness to identify myself with the Object" (*Friend*,I,521n: see also CL,IV, 974-75). In Coleridge's later poems, the poet is moving away from love for natural objects (such as Sara Hutchinson or his own Phantom self) and toward an objectless love, uniting the various aspects of temporal love. But as thinking

---

[1] The distinction between Reason and Understanding is effectively presented in Owen Barfield, *What Coleridge Thought*, pp. 92-114.

is not the same as a thought, and the process of imagining cannot be equated with an imagined poem, so abstracting is not to be confused with *mere* abstractions, the lifeless forms of a dogmatic mind. In his quest for Being, Coleridge found that he needed a new and more "substantial" language that could correspond with his "substantial" self. He needed to create a poetry of abstraction, and make "Love" into a "mode of Being" (CL,III,304).

The task required more than simply resisting the encroachment of physical nature with its Phantom metaphors. The poet needed somehow to resurrect the *life* in words like "Love" and "Hope" and "Duty," to reclaim his own personal experience that had provided language its reason for Being. Thinking was the process by which he hoped to do this, and the physical world could be of little help in returning him to the original unity of thought and thing, the "one life" that he had shattered by "abstruse research." As poetry must be used to reach beyond poetry, abstraction must be used to go beyond abstraction: the Supreme Being was the destination for both poetry and abstraction. The mind he had "denaturalized" (CL,II,725) and painfully confronted in "Dejection: An Ode" suffered a dissociation of sensibility: "partly from ill-health, & partly from an unhealthy & reverie-like vividness of *Thoughts*, & . . . a diminished Impressibility from *Things*, my ideas, wishes, & feelings are to a diseased degree disconnected from *motion* & *action*. In plain & natural English, I am a dreaming & therefore an indolent man" (CL,II,782). The poet must will himself back into motion, avoiding the distorting falsehoods of mere thoughts or mere things. Abstraction became Coleridge's chief "instrument" of Being (*Friend*,I,521), a means of passing beyond the Phantom world and its *Things*.

Having been conditioned by Ezra Pound (and perhaps Hulme and Fenollosa), many modern poets and readers are wary of abstractions in poetry, and insist on "no ideas but in things." Thoughts must be grounded in the "concrete" and the familiar. Pound wrote: "language is made out of concrete things. General expressions in non-concrete terms are a laziness; they are talk, not art, not creation."[2] And another critic, blaming Coleridge's decline on his "neglect of the image," expresses what seems to be a general attitude: "there can be no reconciliation of the opposed modes of expression indicated by the terms 'abstraction' and 'imagination'; and the only possibility of a philosophical or metaphysical *poetry* is a transformation of abstractions into concrete images."[3] This modern predilection, in some instances an obsession, is countered by a considerable body of poetry from the past, including the work of Sidney, Spenser, and Herbert. Believing that man and his language should be evolving into a higher state, Coleridge could never sanction a downward movement, "a transformation of abstraction into concrete images." The poet's life in poetry demonstrates that the dichotomy is not absolute, and both reason *and* imagination are capable of rescuing man from the "despotism of the eye" and creating an "ideal object" that can lead man toward ideal Being. Coleridge wrote that man must "secure himself from the delusive notion, that what is not *imageable* is likewise not *conceivable*. To emancipate the mind from the despotism of the eye is the first step towards the emancipation from the influences and intrusions of the senses, sensations and passions generally."[4] Abstraction can be a repository for experience, a "form for feeling," and a means of discovering a new self.

In order to respond to the abstractions that characterize Coleridge's later work we might look back at his early poems full of bravado and false rhetoric. In the first act of *The Fall of Robespierre*, for example, generalities and abstractions such as Liberty, Conscience, and Freedom seem like empty tokens moved about in a series of verbal exercises, and the endings of descriptive poems are often uncon-

[2] Quoted in Herbert Read, *The True Voice of Feeling: Studies in English Romantic Poetry* (London: Faber & Faber, 1938), p. 126.

[3] Read, pp. 111-12.

[4] Alice D. Snyder, *Coleridge on Logic and Learning*, pp. 126-27.

vincing, such as that of "Reflections on Having Left a Place of Retirement":

> I therefore go, and join head, heart, and hand,
> Active and firm, to fight the bloodless fight
> Of Science, Freedom, and the Truth in Christ.
>
> (PW,I,108)

Likewise, in the early lyrics, following in the manner of Cowper and mid-eighteenth century poets, Coleridge often used stock abstraction to hide his lack of strong personal feeling. The sestet of one sonnet begins "Ah such is Hope!" indicating that the preceding natural description exists only to serve a preconception. Even when abstractions appeared in figurative contexts they remain separate, unabsorbed, lifeless. At sixteen, Coleridge acknowledged his loss of Hope, and at nineteen he confronted Despair, lamenting his loss of Health and Innocence. He faced "Hope's twilight ray" (PW,I,48) long before he became addicted to opium, suffered the hardships of a poor marriage, or endured the pangs of his unconsummated love for Sara Hutchinson. The words appeared before his life had given them substantial meaning. *Life* itself was a mere abstraction.

But by the time of the *Annus Mirabilis*, Coleridge had grown conscious of the unreality and insubstantiality of terms that have not been, as Keats said, "proved on the pulses,"

> Terms which we trundle smoothly o'er our tongues
> Like mere abstractions, empty sounds to which
> We join no feeling and attach no form!
> As if the soldier died without a wound;
> As if the fibers of this godlike frame
> Were gored without a pang; as if the wretch,
> Who fell in battle, doing bloody deeds,
> Passed off to Heaven, translated and not killed."
>
> (PW,I,260)

These lines from "Fears in Solitude" indicate the poet's

awareness of his need to create in language a means of sharing that soldier's pain and also of making the feeling tolerable through authentic "form." Phantom abstractions, like Phantom images, can be evasions of reality and, if not endowed with true feeling, can be as dead as the outer world of nature without a shaping spirit of imagination. Far from falling into empty abstractions, Coleridge was steadily bringing abstractions into the service of Being. By the time of his *Biographia Literaria*, the poet knew the vacancy hidden behind much of his own talk, and he condemned the "pseudo-poesy" that includes "apostrophes to abstract terms. Such are the Odes to Jealousy, to Hope, to Oblivion, and the like" (BL,ɪɪ,66). And he was never to forget that a thought is not necessarily superior to a thing, if it too threatens to confine authentic Being, if "our vitiated imaginations would refine away language to mere abstractions."[5] To the end, the poet held that a true system "should not be grounded in an *abstraction, nor in a Thing*" (CL,ɪv,917). Being is revealed when "extremes meet" in the mind's act of abstracting itself from all objects, whether these be dead language objects (mere abstractions) or objects of sense (mere images).

In one of his important later poems, "Constancy to an Ideal Object" (PW,ɪ,455), Coleridge used his experience of a phenomenon called the "Brocken-Spectre" as an introduction to his meditation on the difficulty of reconciling things and thoughts, a subject with its desired object.[6] Numerous accounts have been given of the Brocken-Spectre, but the poet's own description will serve well: "this refers to a curious phaenomenon which occurs occasionally when the air is filled with fine particles of frozen snow constituting an

[5] Quoted in William Walsh, *Coleridge: The Work and the Relevance* (London: Chatto & Windus, 1967), p. 83.

[6] The Brocken-Spectre and Coleridge's poem are discussed in Stephen Prickett's *Coleridge and Wordsworth: The Poetry of Growth* (Cambridge: Cambridge University Press, 1970), pp. 22-45. I hope to add to Prickett's meaningful discussion.

almost invisible subtle snow-mist, and a person walking with the Sun behind his back. His shadow is projected and he sees a figure moving before him with a glory round its head. I myself have seen it twice" (AR,220).[7] As early as 1799, Coleridge transcribed an account of the Spectre into a note-book (CN,I,430), and he continued to be fascinated by this curious mingling of Phantom and fact. Early vowing to get to the "bottom of the whole mystery," Coleridge wanted to prove that the Spectre was either real or fictive, but be-cause the phenomenon evoked his most intimate doubts about Being (his "negative Being") any resolution of the conflict that he could make seemed arbitrary, a "toy" of the understanding. Even his own poetic treatment of the Spec-tre in "Constancy to an Ideal Object" reached no satisfying conclusion: many things could be *perceived*, but the mys-tery of Being remained behind in the mind that *conceives*.

Coleridge carried the vision of the Brocken-Spectre into other situations, for it was a demonstration of the mind's power to transfigure actuality, and such power was one of his paramount ideas. In a Methodist chapel, with the sun shining on a wall, he noticed how "each spectator opposite would see his own shadow with a heavenly glory, & all the rest dark & rayless" (CN,III,3466). This "glory," or saint's nimbus, must have suggested to him the light of Being that the unbelieving call a myth or fiction. Although he had only momentary glimpses of that light, he knew that the poet's role was to resurrect it from dead forms, of whatever kind. As we have seen with his poems "Phantom" and "Apologia Pro Vita Sua," Coleridge aspired to liberate Being from the "accidents" of temporal existence, to emancipate his eyes from "the black shapeless accidents of size." He believed that the physical world apprehended through the senses lacks true substance and that images are undependable rep-resentatives of Being, but the poet does not consequently escape into abstraction. The Brocken-Spectre caused one of

[7] Coleridge's annotation to *Aids to Reflection* (1825). B.M.C. 134 c.10.

those meetings of opposites that unsettles the understanding
and prepares the way for Being.

### Constancy to an Ideal Object

Since all that beat about in Nature's range,
Or veer or vanish; why should'st thou remain
The only constant in a world of change,
O yearning Thought! that liv'st but in the brain?
Call to the Hours, that in the distance play,
The faery people of the future day—
Fond Thought! not one of all that shining swarm
Will breathe on thee with life-enkindling breath,
Till when, like strangers shelt'ring from a storm,
Hope and Despair meet in the porch of Death!
Yet still thou haunt'st me; and though well I see,
She is not thou, and only thou art she,
Still, still as though some dear embodied Good,
Some living Love before my eyes there stood
With answering look a ready ear to lend,
I mourn to thee and say—"Ah! loveliest friend!
That this the meed of all my toils might be,
To have a home, an English home, and thee!"
Vain repetition! Home and Thou are one.
The peacefull'st cot, the moon shall shine upon,
Lulled by the thrush and wakened by the lark,
Without thee were but a becalméd bark,
Whose Helmsman on an ocean waste and wide
Sits mute and pale his mouldering helm beside.

And art thou nothing? Such thou art, as when
The woodman winding westward up the glen
At wintry dawn, where o'er the sheep-track's maze
The viewless snow-mist weaves a glist'ning haze,
Sees full before him, gliding without tread,
An image with a glory round its head;
The enamoured rustic worships its fair hues,
Nor knows he makes the shadow, he pursues!

(PW,I,455-56)

In "Constancy to an Ideal Object" Coleridge combines the mist and the sun, a human perceiver and his projected shadow, to create an interrelationship whose "meaning" is weakened when we reduce the poem to a summarizing statement: e.g., the poet's fictions are exposed as counterfeit. As with *The Ancient Mariner*, Coleridge's conclusion can be misleading; it gives the impression that the Brocken-Spectre is simply a metaphor intended to teach us how to behave in the world. The poet's final question, followed by an "answer" that is truly an extended simile, leads the reader to believe that a categorical choice has been made: man is either a phantom or a fact, a deluded dreamer or an impoverished realist. But the questions and doubts of the haunted mind behind the poem remain, and Coleridge's dictum that we should distinguish but not divide is useful here in considering mind and world. Reflection, with its dual meaning of meditation and self-mirroring, may lead to death, as we saw with Narcissus and the pool of nature, but when reflection focuses on an *ideal* object a reconciliation of opposites is possible and a new identity can be conceived. By distinguishing the subject from its desired object, the poet makes of his *desire* an object for meditation: he begins to know himself. Coleridge's ending does not provide a statement that resolves the continual conflict between mere abstraction, a "yearning Thought! that liv'st but in the brain," and the *élan vital* outside that yearns to transcend the limitations of matter. Both would unite in the "one life," just as the poet and the thinker seek to unite in a Being that transcends restricting labels. The "rival conflict," as Coleridge called the relationship between mind and external nature, must end in armistice, not peace. Once more, Owen Barfield alerts us to a difficulty that continually faces some readers of Coleridge: "it is the inexorable presupposition in the minds of his readers, that whatever is not a thing *must* be an abstraction, which, more than perhaps anything else, has prevented his system from being understood."[8] A

8 Owen Barfield, *What Coleridge Thought*, p. 24.

thought that "liv'st but in the brain" is only half alive, and a natural object without a governing consciousness is an "idol of sense," a Phantom, a devitalized *it*.

Coleridge's love for Sara Hutchinson that could not find its "outness" in physical expression is clearly the underlying impulse that brings about the philosophical debate over how and what one can know in "Constancy to an Ideal Object." As a poet, Coleridge is committed to the ideal, abstract world; consequently, his ideal object is the *thought* of Sara rather than her physical presence, it is *love* and not love's embodiment. The personal speech directed to the woman, in which the poet expresses his need for a particular "English home, and thee," fits into a larger, general context in which the speaker must find his consolation, if not his ultimate fulfillment. For Coleridge, that context is more poetic than philosophical, for as he said in the *Biographia Literaria*: "it is not less an essential mark of true genius, that its sensibility is excited by any other cause more powerfully than by its own personal interests; for this plain reason, that the man of genius lives most in the ideal world, in which the present is still constituted by the future or the past" (BL,I, 30). Despite the record of his own failed ideal objects, Coleridge refused to accept his Being as a series of disparate, unrelated moments. "Without Memory," he wrote, "there can be no hope—the Present is a phantom known only by it's pining, if it do not breathe the vital air of the Future: and what is the Future, but the Image of the Past projected on the mist of the Unknown, and seen with a glory round it's head" (CL,v,266). Coleridge's memory would not permit him to live in Blake's "eternal sunrise": he needed to recover what he had lost. Past, present, and future "Blend" or "modify each other," but the poet must continually project himself into eternity. Memory produces knowledge and, in fact, is the "Great Guide of Things to come, Sole Presence of Things Past" (CN,II,3089). However, Coleridge's frequent inability to progress in time, to see through nature to the Being within objects, was the cause of his recurring despair.

Like his other late poems of dejection, "Constancy to an Ideal Object" presents the poet in a stagnant condition. When he invokes the "Hours" at the beginning of the poem, he denies the possibility of a future; several lines later, thought cannot generate "life-enkindling breath"; and finally, unable to imagine a world without Sara, the poet, like his Mariner, is in a "becalméd bark" upon "an ocean waste and wide." He must, through poetry, create an abstraction or an "object" that can inspire movement, a "fond Thought" that can replace the unattainable fond Sara. Like Eliot in "Ash-Wednesday," Coleridge cannot find satisfaction within nature and must "construct something/ Upon which to rejoice." The woman who exists in a world of change must be redefined, given a life beyond "Nature's range," a life made visible in art, which Coleridge defined (by way of Schelling) as "a middle quality between a thought and a thing . . . the union and reconciliation of that which is nature with that which is exclusively human" (BL,II,254-55). By remaking Sara, Coleridge was recreating himself. As Keats said, that which is creative must create itself.

The abstractions in "Constancy to an Ideal Object," distinguished from the abstracting process that is the poem itself, function as that "middle quality" and become by Coleridge's definition "symbolic": they "partake of the reality they render intelligible." By means of the poet's enlivening imagination, love becomes "living Love" and good becomes "embodied Good." But here the poet's doubts will not allow him the pure apprehension of Being he enjoyed in "Phantom." Haunted by the *thought* of Sara, he is clearly aware that "She is not thou, and only thou art she." The poet's evident struggle to make his pronoun designations consistent may be a symptom of his greater struggle to bring image into abstraction. Of the ten uses of the intimate form (thee or thou), six clearly refer to the poet's Thought, "she" being reserved for the physical woman. But halfway through the poem, a metamorphosis takes place. The poet begins to embody Thought (II.13-14) so that the speech that follows is directed at the individual woman and the familiar "thou" is assigned to her three times. Moreover, the only capitalized "Thou" in the poem occurs when the person is elevated to the abstract level by being identified with another thought ("Home and Thou are one"). After considerable wavering, Coleridge's final use of "thou" appears to include both Sara and the Thought-of-Sara.

Employing a metaphoric identity, a mere metaphor as a "conventional exponent of a thing," could prevent Coleridge from proceeding toward that ideal conception of the self that he sought. Making an equation, using the simple verb to be, is not the same as evoking Being. Only through symbol and paradox ("She is not thou, and only thou art she") can the poet begin the process of transformation that leads to Being. Abstractions as well as objects *live* for Coleridge, and he acknowledges this life even when he denies its attainability, just as he accepts the existence of God although he often cannot reach Him through the language of prayer. Characteristically, Coleridge tries to objectify himself by means of another person, as he did with the old man in "Limbo." He would convert Sara into a *living idea*, neither a generalization drawn from phenomena nor a cold Cartesian abstraction. The Thought is clearly not Sara, but the only Sara that Coleridge can enjoy is *in* Thought. His frustration furthers self-realization; his feeling takes form through his "act and power of abstracting the thoughts and images from their original cause, and of reflecting on them with less and less reference to the individual suffering that had been their first subject" (Shedd,iv,435).

If we could accept Coleridge as a pure idealist, a man who chose Berkeley over Hartley and never looked back, we might merge the poet with his "enamoured rustic" and assert that both were victims of illusion. But we cannot ignore the history of Coleridge's mind-nature conflict, which was unresolved from beginning to end. In 1825 he still viewed them as rival artists and feared that nature "is sure to get the better of Lady Mind—in the long run." Despite his playful tone here, he indicates those difficult periods of his life when nature "mocks the mind with it's own metaphors" (CL,v,497). Surely Coleridge was no "rustic," as his comments on Wordsworth's peasants in the *Biographia Literaria* emphasize, for the poet reasoned that a rustic's limited mind is incapable of abstracting, that he sees only an image and rests ignorant of Being. Through his power of mind, Coleridge could see the negative possibilities in the Brocken-Spectre:

> O! Superstition is the Giant Shadow
> Which the Solicitude of weak Mortality
> Its Back toward Religion's rising Sun,
> Casts on the thin mist of the uncertain Future.
>
> (CN,III,4283)

In "Constancy to an Ideal Object" the poet is perhaps ambivalent, praising innocence while ridiculing the superstitious Woodman who, unaware that art and nature can collaborate, seems to worship a Phantom that is neither God nor external nature. He resembles other men who tend "to break and scatter the one divine and invisible life of nature into countless idols of the sense" (*Friend*,I,518). Coleridge at once believes that no picture can stand for a living idea, but nevertheless the phenomenon must be seen before it can be understood. Knowledge grows out of a continuum, for "without seeing, we should never *know* (i.e. know ourselves to have known) that we had Eyes" (CL,v,97). Striving for a higher consciousness, Coleridge may be further using the Woodman to embody that aspect of himself which was tempted to dream beneath the mystic's "Cloud of Unknowing." As a very young man, Coleridge had said, "I never regarded *my senses* in any way as the criteria of my belief" (CL,I,354), and yet he labored with scientific precision throughout his lifetime to analyze sensory data. His two idols, Plato and Shakespeare, "were not visionaries, nor mystics; but dwelt in 'the sober certainty' of waking knowledge" (TM,38), and in his very late work, *Aids to Reflec-*

*tion*, mysticism is thoroughly condemned. The "enamoured rustic" sees and makes unconsciously, but the poet knows he makes. His willing suspension of disbelief allows him to unite his power with the power in nature to create a glorified phenomenon, a revelation of Being.

Coleridge's question, "And art thou nothing?" is certainly not rhetorical, despite the subsequent lines that seem to offer the clarifying answer and meaning. The poet questions not only the self he has created but, moreover, the work of art in which that self momentarily appears. Are you no physical thing? Are you a mere abstraction? Are you a man divested of meaning, "nothing's anomaly!"? Are you, perhaps, the "limbus" of Paracelsus out of which positive Being can emerge? The whole poem, rather than the concluding assertion alone, provides the poet's answer. He has attempted to take a person, a noun, a thing existing in space and time, a *Sara*, and by means of thought to transform her into an ideal object worthy of adoration: "the only constant in a world of change." But as we have already seen, Coleridge was continually suspended between thoughts and things. His own opposing selves can meet in a poem, but one cannot fully dominate the other. Coleridge links with a conjunction the two abstractions Hope and Despair, but they are not unified, for they embody Coleridge's two *realities* of feeling, his positive and negative Being. Only in death will their conflict be ended. They will meet in the "porch" of death, just as Coleridge always found himself just outside the house of Being, "on the threshold of some Joy, that cannot be entered into while I am embodied" (CN,III,3370). Coleridge's ideal object, finally, must not be regarded as an entity but as an act, an act of consciousness that joins opposites without cancelling them out. In contrast to the stagnant, passive Being represented by the "mute" and "pale" Helmsman who cannot progress toward any meaningful goal, the Woodman at the end of the poem is filled with Hope, and the final lines of the poem register activity, an energy that makes thought vital: the Woodman is "winding" his way through nature as its invisible power "weaves" the haze that separates us from ultimate meaning. The image the Woodman sees is also "gliding," and while celebrating his object he "pursues" it. The underscored vitality of Coleridge's language (winding, weaving, gliding, pursues) contrasts pointedly with the static, nominative character of the poem's title, "Constancy to an Ideal Object."

Like "Frost at Midnight," whose ending marries created and creating nature, "Constancy to an Ideal Object" unites the meditative mind and its object of meditation. Through the "life-enkindling" power of the poet's imagination, his abstractions are reclaimed from pure thought and returned to the life that fostered them. Coleridge speculated that the mind is a verb and the body a substantive, but in his poem he created a remarkable combination, the "Verb substantive" (CN,III,4412). The act of seeing in itself cannot be a means of discovering Being, and neither can the act of thinking if it is divorced from experience. In nature we may find only shapeless accidents, and in the mind only counterfeits. Art, however, can bring thoughts and things—experience itself—into a temporary form, a shape for Being. In a work of art, the imaginative viewer can discover both himself and his transfigured self:

> In the plays of Shakespeare every man sees himself, without knowing that he does so: as in some of the phenomena of nature, in the mist of the mountain, the traveller beholds his own figure, but the glory round the head distinguishes it from a mere vulgar copy. In traversing the Brocken, in the north of Germany, at sunrise, the brilliant beams are shot askance, and you see before you a being of gigantic proportions, and of such elevated dignity, that you only know it to be yourself by similarity of action. In the same way, near Messina, natural forms, at determined distances, are represented on an invisible mist, not as they really exist, but dressed in all the prismatic colours of the imagina-

tion. So in Shakespeare: every form is true, everything
has reality for its foundation; we can all recognize
the truth, but we see it decorated with such hues of
beauty, and magnified to such proportions of grandeur,
that, while we know the figure, we know also how much
it has been refined and exalted by the poet. (ShC,ii,163)

Perhaps the rustic Woodman in approaching either nature
or Shakespeare "sees himself, without knowing that he does
so," but Coleridge's quotation significantly ends with a kind
of waking knowledge that extends beyond self-deception:
"while we know the figure, we know also how much it has
been refined and exalted by the poet." The work of art may
be a record of the meeting between a perceiving mind and
external nature, but only when the viewer refuses to choose
between the presented opposites, and accepts Being as a by-
product of the meeting, is a new consciousness possible.
Abstraction may be what Coleridge calls an "instrument"
of Being, but abstract knowledge is a falsehood when "we
think of ourselves as separated beings, and place nature in
antithesis to the mind, as object to subject, thing to thought,
death to life. This is abstract knowledge, or the science of
the mere understanding" (*Friend*,i,520-21). Being, like nature itself, is forever about to be born. Opposites serve to
demonstrate their interdependence. The ideal object is finally not an object, but a subject that has been realized:
"the I is not an object; but a self-affirmed act—and if it will
not believe itself, what or whom can it believe?" (CN,iii,
4356).

Coleridge knew that whenever he stopped believing in
his own power he became an object and his self-evolution
ceased, for "all that is truly human must proceed from
within" (PL,226). The significant number of despairing
poems that the poet wrote in his later years indicates the
difficulty of self-affirmation when the outside world provides no self-reflection. In his negative moods, Coleridge
viewed the world as a prison house and he suspected that
all objects, including himself, were without any transfigur-

ing glory.[9] As with Eliot later, the earth's annual renewal served as a painful reminder of his own arrested growth, his own failure to unite spiritual and natural evolution. The "yearly resurrection of Nature" could not fill Coleridge with joy because of his own "past procrastination, and cowardly impatience of pain" (CL,VI,571-72). Nature's "inexhaustible" forms can be exhausting to man if he is incapable of regenerating himself, when abstraction fails him as an "instrument" of Being. Like his Helmsman in the "becalméd bark," Coleridge needed some "living Love" to rescue him from despair. Through language, he had to create the object that the world did not provide. His poem "Work Without Hope" attempts to rejuvenate the abstraction "Hope" and thereby restore direction to his evolutionary movement.

The version of "Work Without Hope" that appears in one of Coleridge's letters (21 February 1825) differs a great deal from the one published in the *Bijou* in 1828, which came to be the standard text. Again, as with "Limbo," the poem has been separated from its evolutionary background and cut by more than half. The published version reveals in the first stanza a burgeoning earth and a speaker unable to engage in the process of living; and in the second stanza, an ideal world from which he is also alienated. As in other reverie or Limbo poems, the speaker is half awake and his "drowsy" Soul lacks the power to initiate spiritual growth. Knowing that he does not belong to Phantom nature (which only "seems" at work) the poet has not yet turned the abstraction Hope into "living Hope," and it too resembles an "unbusy Thing." That "Work Without Hope" appears rather frequently in selections of Coleridge poems indicates, perhaps, either some admiration for the superficial form of

---

[9] In *The Prelude* Wordsworth laments Coleridge's condition: "The self-created sustenance of a mind/ Debarred from Nature's living images" (VI,201-05). I see Coleridge in a more positive way. By rejecting nature's consoling images, the poet makes possible the creation of "a bodiless substance, an unborrow'd self."

the poem with its neatly balanced structure, or some sympathy for the pathetic voice. Like "Constancy to an Ideal Object," the poem can be interpreted as another demonstration of Coleridge's frustrated love for Sara Hutchinson.

By returning to Coleridge's original lines and his prose introduction, we find that from the beginning Coleridge avoided the limitations of the personal confessional mode by creating another speaker for his lines: the Biblical Jacob. We also find that although the poem deals with Love, Coleridge is less concerned with finding a physical object for his affections than he is in becoming, in the words of one of his *Shakespeare Lectures*, "a secondary creator of himself" (ShC,II,142). His love for Sara, transposed into Jacob's love for Leah, must eventually be elevated to a higher realm of abstraction where the subject and the object are subsumed by Love itself, by absolute Being. Although the opening stanza of "Work Without Hope" seems to suggest that the phenomenal world was a possible "object" for the poet, the longer version reveals that, on the contrary, nature works to prevent self-realization. Earlier, Coleridge's two images, an Aeolian harp and its breeze, represented two complementary forces that produced harmonious music. In his later years, however, nature became an antagonist. We can never say of Coleridge what was said of Wordsworth, that "the life of the mind was wholly projected upon external nature."[10]

## Work Without Hope

All Nature seems at work. Slugs leave their lair;
The Bees are stirring; Birds are on the wing;
And WINTER slumb'ring in the open air
Wears on his smiling face a dream of Spring.
And I, the while, the sole unbusy Thing,
Nor honey make, nor pair, nor build, nor sing.

[10] David Perkins, *The Quest for Permanence* (Cambridge, Mass.: Harvard University Press, 1969), p. 59.

Yet well I ken the banks, where Amaranths blow,
Have traced the fount whence streams of Nectar flow.
Bloom, O ye Amaranths! bloom for whom ye may—
For me ye bloom not! Glide, rich Streams! Away!
With unmoist Lip and wreathless Brow I stroll:
And would you learn the Spells, that drowse my Soul?
WORK without Hope draws nectar in a sieve;
And HOPE without an Object cannot live.
I speak in figures, inward thoughts and woes
Interpreting by Shapes and outward Shews.
Call the World Spider: and at fancy's touch
Thought becomes image and I see it such.
With viscous masonry of films and threads
Tough as the Nets in Indian Forests found
It blends the Waller's and the Weaver's trades
And soon the tent-like Hangings touch the ground—
A dusky chamber that excludes the Day—
But cease the prelude & resume the lay.

Where daily nearer me (with magic Ties,
Line over line & thick'ning as they rise)
The World her spidery threads on all sides spun,
Side answ'ring Side with narrow interspace,
My Faith (say I: I and my Faith are one)
Hung, as a Mirror there! And face to face
(For nothing else there was, between or near)
One Sister Mirror hid the dreary Wall.
But *That* is broke! And with that bright Compeer
I lost my Object and my inmost All—
Faith *in* the Faith of THE ALONE MOST DEAR!

Jacob Hodiernus
(early version: CL,v,415-16)

In Coleridge's letter he announces that he has been thinking about a "self-conscious Looking-glass," an emblem of the subject-object duality that he must engage before he can begin to move toward ideal Being. As he further speculates on the possibility of "two such Looking-glasses fronting, each seeing the other in itself, and itself in the other," we realize that the natural world can now serve only as background for the process of self-realization: the self must ultimately confront itself. Coleridge may not have agreed with Blake that "where man is absent, nature is barren," but he avoided using nature as a reflecting pool, and the myth of Narcissus became a constant warning that self-consciousness and self-fulfillment had to be willed into Being. And perhaps this explains Coleridge's use of the strikingly artificial "mirror" within nature as a means of abstracting himself in order to define that Love which can "outlive all change save a change with regard to itself." The world with its images spreads a spider web that blocks out the light of Being, but the poet's abstracting mind, when "Thought becomes image," can create an equally inhospitable, windowless house that "excludes the Day." In contrast to the active, "stirring" earth in the published version of the poem, the original version contains no appealing images of physical nature; in fact, nature prevents man from finding his own "reflex." Because Coleridge had exposed the world as a Phantom, he was unwilling to "value its Shews," its misleading consolations. His idea of Love, so intimately related to his idea of Being, could not find expression very long in objects in time and space. He would probably have agreed with Eliot that "Love is most nearly itself/ When here and now cease to matter."

Jacob was the persona that Coleridge assumed but then edited out of the printed poem, and rather than "Work Without Hope" the original version is called *"The Alone Most Dear*: a Complaint of Jacob to Rachel as in the tenth year of his Service he saw in her or *fancied* he saw Symptoms of Alienation." For Coleridge, Jacob probably represented as well as any human being the virtue of Constancy to an Ideal Object. His labors in the temporal world acquired their value through an abstraction, Hope, and his very life embodied the abstraction, since union with his physical love object was perpetually postponed. Any ideal object is, per se, beyond time and space; hence it can only be defined by the ardor of the pursuer. Unlike Sisyphus, Jacob is being tested, not punished, but Coleridge must have felt that as a man he was being both tested and punished by God. The poet's frustration and pain seemed inexplicable until he realized that they might be essential to his evolution toward Being, that "our misery may be a merciful mode of recalling us from our Self-chosen Exile" (CN,III,4341). Both Jacob and Coleridge learned the power of Hope. In a letter Coleridge wrote in his final year to a young couple anticipating marriage, he recommended that they ask themselves: "do I possess that moral fortitude, that cheerfulness of Hope, which will not only *neutralize* 'the Delay that maketh the heart sick,' but convert it into an incentive to perseverant exertion—for without this, the best years of life might be wasted away in day-dreams of feeble love-yearning—in sad contrast with the patriarch of old. 'And Jacob served seven years for Rachel: and they seemed to him but a few days, for the love he had to her'" (CL,VI,878-79). Although more than one reader might describe Coleridge's life as "wasted away in day-dreams of feeble love-yearning," the picture is inaccurate because his vast body of writing proves his "perseverant exertion" in evolving Love from "love-yearning." In his poem he both acknowledges his own weaknesses, his tendency toward self-pity, and demonstrates, through Jacob's ordeal, that *patience is an act*, and Hope a way of Life.

In his introductory remarks to the original "Work Without Hope," Coleridge characterized his "self-conscious Looking-glass" as a product of the fancy rather than the imagination. Yet both the fancy and the understanding can be "substance-declaring," even when they cannot effect those integrations of opposites achieved by the reason and the imagination.[11] The almost surrealistic placing of one

[11] "This is the true import of the word, Understanding. It is the *substantiating*, substance-declaring, Power. When, however, we pro-

mirror to face the other seems a deliberate distortion of the traditional mirroring of nature. In any case, the mirror must be broken before the poet can become aware that self-integration can only be achieved by the self in isolation from nature. That the "Sister Mirror" represents Sara Hutchinson indicates Coleridge's persistent need to abstract himself from his immediate problems, for the poet's concept of sister love (like his recurring mother-child image) aims at de-sensualizing feeling and diminishing the power of an *object*, either as a person or as a poetic image. The poet grows conscious of ideal Love when he finds himself alone in the universe, in which glorified nature is only a "dreary wall" and physical love is not even a diversion from approaching despair:

> One Sister Mirror hid the dreary Wall.
> But *That* is broke! And with that bright Compeer
> I lost my Object and my inmost All—
> Faith *in* the Faith of THE ALONE MOST DEAR!

Both nature and art produce only counterfeits of Being, and so the self must create its own object in which to express its Being: "The Alone Most Dear," whether for Jacob or Coleridge, exists in the mind as an "inward Thought" of an "inmost All." Coleridge was ever alert to the danger of confounding God and nature—the Stoics "confounded God and Nature. For this was the grand error of Socrates himself" (PL,219-20)—and the poet realized that any identity had to be achieved through a living abstraction: "I and my Faith are one."

The name signing the poem, "Jacob Hodiernus," is another instance of Coleridge's need to project his personal

---

ceed under the influence of the Fancy, and not according to the rules of the Understanding, the Product or Result is an Hypo*poiesis* not an Hypo*thesis*, a Suf*fiction* not a Supposition" (CL,v,468).

suffering onto a surrogate, thus abstracting himself from his problem. In his early youth he had written, "Love is a local anguish" (CL,1,88), but the poems of his later years such as "Work Without Hope" testify to the poet's desire to find a new definition that would free him from the "local" and urge him toward absolute Being: "the absolute is neither singly that which affirms, nor that which is affirmed; but the identity and living copula of both" (*Friend*,1,521). The loss of faith in one of God's creatures should never destroy man's faith in God, for He can make "The whole one Self! Self, that no alien knows!" (PW,1,115). If Jacob did detect "Symptoms of Alienation" in Rachel as he came close to attaining her, he never appears to have deserted his "inmost All." He perhaps exemplifies Coleridge's idea of genius: "genius to live in the universal, to know no self but that which is reflected not only from the faces of all around us, our fellow creatures, but reflected from the flowers, the trees, the beasts, yea from the very surface of the waters and the sands of the desert. A man of genius finds a reflex of himself, were it only in the mystery of Being" (PL,179). But as "Work Without Hope" demonstrates, particularly in its early version, Coleridge was not often capable of enjoying the physical world as a reflection of God, as did St. John of the Cross, or of enjoying human love as a satisfying metaphor for divine love.

Many of Coleridge's later poems act as evidence that one can Work Without Hope. But then the work is in finding a new meaning for the abstraction, in finding an appropriate object for a Hope that had been misdirected and misunderstood. At the time of his break with Sara Hutchinson in 1810 (about fifteen years before "Work Without Hope"), Coleridge was devastated, unable even to imagine that she was not the "Bodiless substance" and the "unborrow'd self" he was looking for. Having identified his self with his projected self, and his love with the physical object of love, Coleridge's precarious sense of Being had been shattered.

Like a widower, he became distraught, unable to rid himself
of that self-indulgence which prevents self-consciousness:

> I have experienc'd
> The worst, the World can wreak on me; the worst
> That can make Life indifferent, yet disturb
> With whisper'd Discontents the dying prayer.
> I have beheld the whole of all, wherein
> My Heart had any interest in this Life,
> To be disrent and torn from off my Hopes,
> That nothing now is left. Why then live on?
> That Hostage, which the world had in its keeping
> Given by me as a Pledge that I would live,
> That Hope of Her, say rather, that pure Faith
> In her fix'd Love, which held me to keep truce
> With the Tyranny of Life—is gone ah whither?
> What boots it to reply?—" 'tis gone! and now
> Well may I break this Pact, this League, of Blood
> That ties me to myself—and break I shall"—
>
> (CN,III,3796)

By making Sara "the whole of all" Coleridge had short cir-
cuited his developing line of self-evolution: a line that
should have progressed from the personal to the Absolute
self. By falsely equating Being with the body, which is its
confining form, he had almost committed the sin of confounding the Creator with His creation. The poet, with his
mirror object shattered, seems incapable of resurrecting
Being from the body as he had done earlier in "Phantom."
As in his verse letter that became "Dejection: An Ode,"
only a moral obligation to his children, his "league of
blood," stands between him and suicide, the ultimate despairing act. What Coleridge did not realize at the time was
that he had painfully broken off from the *object as object*,
and that such a break was necessary before his abstractions
(Love, Hope, Faith) could realize their universal meaning.
The despair that he experienced was counterfeit, for as

Kierkegaard wrote, "despair is not the loss of the beloved, that is misfortune, pain, suffering; but despair is the lack of the eternal."[12]

Coleridge raged against the limitations of phenomenal form, but he had already written his way out of true despair, even before the tragic experience. But this experience had authenticated the words: "and now, that I am alone, & utterly hopeless for myself—yet still *I love*—& more strongly than ever feel that Conscience, or the Duty of Love, is the Proof of continuing, as it is the Cause & Condition of existing, Consciousness" (CN,II,3231). As we have seen before, Coleridge's abstractions had to assume meaning within the poet's life, but before they could he had to redirect his goal beyond space and time. At the time of the break with Sara, he confronted an anguishing possibility: "Horrid Thought! it seems as if I alone of all men had *Love!* as if it were a sense, a faculty to which there was no corresponding Object!—Oct. 29. 1810—" (CN,III,3998). But in the end (and before the end) Coleridge discovered that he was not alone, and that he had mistaken Phantom objects for real ones. Perhaps Sara realized that she had been to Coleridge not so much a woman as "an image with a glory round its head." Perhaps all artists use the world and its inhabitants as materials out of which they create a new consciousness, a new awareness of Being:

> . . . strange and generous self! there can only be such a self by a complete divestment of all that men call self, —of all that can make it either practically to others, or consciously to the individual himself, different from the human race in its ideal. Such self is but a perpetual religion, an inalienable acknowledgement of God, the sole basis and ground of being. In this sense, how can I love God, and not love myself, as far as it is of God?
> (ShC,I,115)

[12] Søren Kierkegaard, *Works of Love*, trans. David F. Swenson and Lillian Marvin Swenson (London: Oxford University Press, 1946), p. 34.

After his break with Sara, Coleridge never again demanded so much from an earthly love object, but he continued to maintain his belief that "feeling is not objectless."
Even though he could picture himself as an Arab that "some
Caravan had left behind" in a desert, he nevertheless knew
that "the very duty must for ever keep alive feelings the
appropriate objects of which are indeed in another world"
(AP,292-93). The poet's friendship with Wordsworth was
superficially restored, but it was only a phantom of the
original. In his constancy to ideal Being, and to the human
language from which poets must attempt to create temporary forms that declare Being, Coleridge turned often in
his later years to the abstraction "Duty" to help him keep
his desire from stagnating as a result of his unsatisfactory
love objects. The poet, rather than suffering "vain regrets,"
chose instead to awaken the authentic power hidden within
conventional abstractions: "Let us do our *Duty*: all else is
a Dream, Life and Death alike a Dream" (CN,II,2537). His
poem "Duty Surviving Self-Love" (PW,I,459-60) may at
first seem to be mere sentimental moralizing, a preacher's
stock phraseology, but here the poet does not escape from
experience into abstraction, he enlists abstraction to give
form to the suffering and disappointment that accompany
earthly activity. Never to have risked the self, never to have
brought Love onto the field of action, was to have remained
at a lower level of evolution toward Being, content with
what he called a "filagree religion" (MC,350). Coleridge
knew that apathetic piety was tantamount to being "without religion because it was without struggle, without difficulty" (CL,II,1008). If the Mariner had never gone to sea,
he might never have comprehended his Duty to Love.

Duty Surviving Self-Love
The only sure friend of declining life
A Soliloquy

Unchanged within, to see all changed without,
Is a blank lot and hard to bear, no doubt.

Yet why at others' wanings should'st thou fret?
Then only might'st thou feel a just regret,
Hadst thou withheld thy love or hid thy light
In selfish forethought of neglect and slight.
O wiselier then, from feeble yearnings freed,
While, and on whom, thou may'st—shine on! nor heed
Whether the object by reflected light
Return thy radiance or absorb it quite:
And though thou notest from thy safe recess
Old Friends burn dim, like lamps in noisome air,
Love them for what they *are*; nor love them less,
Because to thee they are not what they *were*.

(PW,I,459-60; Coleridge's MS emphasis)

Coleridge's "Soliloquy" has, by definition, no responding voice, but it seems to be spoken to that conservative Coleridge who had sometimes sought a "safe recess" from the bombardments of life by accepting conventional forms, whether of behavior or poetry (the behavior of form). Ironically, this poem demonstrates that there can be no sanctuary from suffering, no anodyne to relieve the pain of consciousness. That old friends decay in a decaying world is a fact of existence but not of Being, and the poet can see things as they are by means of "the gift of distance without detachment," a gift that Coleridge said characterized Genius.[13] The "Duty" that survives the failure and death of phenomenal objects (or selves) is a rejuvenating power. The poet has endured his "blank lot" and learned, like Blake's Little Black Boy, "to bear the beams of love." Experience has aided him in evolving a new form for Love, not Eros but Agape, a spiritual shining that encompasses all physical objects but does not depend on them for self-realization. Coleridge faces his disappointment in Wordsworth, among others, starkly and unsentimentally in the line "Old Friends burn dim, like lamps in noisome air," but Duty lives on to

[13] Quoted by Kathleen Coburn, "Coleridge: A Bridge between Science and Poetry," *Coleridge's Variety: Bicentenary Studies*, ed. John Beer (Pittsburgh: University of Pittsburgh Press, 1975), p. 97.

direct the poet toward Being itself. Coleridge suffered through a long history of conflicts, but in the end the struggle strengthened rather than weakened his will. He wrote that "the spirit (originally the identity of object and subject) must in some sense dissolve this identity, in order to be conscious of it: fit alter et idem. But this implies an act, and it follows therefore that intelligence or self-consciousness is impossible, except by and in a will" (BL,i,185). The word Duty does not simply designate proper social behavior —our obligation to others; it first signifies an obligation to the self—our need to distinguish a self existing in time (what we *were*) and the Being that is only revealed through time (what we *are*).

Unlike Wordsworth's "Ode to Duty" in which a conventional abstraction is used to promote conventional morality, Coleridge's poem shows Duty as an energizing power in the service of self-evolution. Coleridge felt that Wordsworth was by a gift of nature invulnerable to destructive forces from without. Because he had always had love he never needed love, and hence his Duty had never been tested. Secure within his domestic peace, Wordsworth could accept the *given* meaning for the abstraction, but Coleridge had to test and recreate Duty since he had severed its connection with conventional morality by leaving his wife and succumbing to opium. He explained his great need: "I have never had any one, in whose Heart and House I could be an Inmate, who loved me enough to take pride & joy in the efforts of my power, being at the same time so by me beloved as to have an influence over my mind. And I am too weak to do my Duty for the Duty's sake" (CL,iii,307). Within Coleridge's more rigorous Christianity, "too weak" may ironically signify that the poet was "too strong" to allow the language of piety to deaden his own consciousness. As we saw earlier with his use of the Eddy metaphor, the self can in its insatiable demands turn in on itself, producing a "hopeless and heartless" condition unless the poet can revitalize Duty or Conscience (the two seem at times nearly synonymous), which are able to rescue man from

Phantoms and guide him toward the absolute. Dejection, or negative Being, came about because Coleridge was incapable of the egotistical sublime. When his abstractions were emptied of their meaning and became worn out words, despair was inevitable: "the effect of *Selfness* in a mind incapable of gross Self-interest—decrease of Hope and Joy, the Soul in its round & round flight forming narrower circles, till at every Gyre its wings beat against the *personal Self*" (CN,II,2531). This need to remake the self is precisely what is lacking in Wordsworth's "Ode to Duty," and his late poems in general. Wordsworth's abstractions (Duty, Justice, Law, Honor) seem like common coin in a passionless exchange. Like the meter that Wordsworth once said was "superadded" to poetry, the poet's abstractions seem superadded to experience, not a living part of it.

Coleridge's "Duty Surviving Self-Love" was written about twenty years after Wordsworth's "Ode to Duty," but curiously it does not display calm resignation before an emptiness that is "hard to bear," but mirrors a mind undergoing the difficult struggle for Being and resisting the temptation to despair. Without naming Duty, Coleridge presents Duty in action defining a life. By the end of his poem, Duty has educated the poet to a Love that transcends self-love and shines on even when the world provides no object for love. Duty frees the poet from his need for temporal satisfaction and prepares him for the light that is to come. In contrast, Wordsworth considers Duty to be a restraining power rather than a liberating one. His abstraction involves law and mandate, discipline by rod, regulation and denial. According to Wordsworth, Love and Joy are not present realities related to Duty but are only possible, it seems, in some future realm "When love is an unerring light,/ And Joy its own security." In the present world, the Joy of Being must be restrained. Coleridge recognized Wordsworth's differing conception of the word Duty when he was driven almost to hysteria by the suspicion that Wordsworth and Sara Hutchinson might be lovers: "it is not the voice, not the duty of *his* nature, to love *any* being as I love you" (CN,II,3148). For Coleridge, Joy and Love are not simply future possibilities, even though he considered them more available to others than to himself. Duty instructs Coleridge to "shine on!"—to declare Being and not repress it. His Duty is to make Love a present, self-affirming act.

In contrast to Coleridge's struggle for Being which continues throughout his life, Wordsworth's late poems express a human condition that seems "without religion because it is without struggle, without difficulty" (CL,II,1008). As John Jones says, "the religion of gratitude makes the imagination everywhere ceremonious."[14] Wordsworth's "Ode to Duty" seeks "control" over emotions that are never out of control:

> Through no disturbance of my soul
> Or strong compunction in me wrought,
> I supplicate for thy control;
> But in the quietness of thought:
> Me this unchartered freedom tires;
> I feel the weight of chance desires:
> My hopes no more must change their name,
> I long for a repose that ever is the same.

At the end of "Ode to Duty," the poet's bemoaning of human weakness seems unconvincing because weakness has not been realized within the poem itself: "Oh, let my weakness have an end!" On the other hand, Coleridge's "Soliloquy" presents the "compunction" that Duty must turn into active love, and includes his existential weakness: his loneliness, his need for people, his self-pity, his bitterness toward a "noisome" world. Wordsworth wrote that "the education of man, and above all a Christian, is the education of *duty*, which is most forcibly taught by the business and concerns of life,"[15] but a sense of immediate life is, for the

---

[14] John Jones, *The Egotistical Sublime: A History of Wordsworth's Imagination* (London: Chatto & Windus, 1954), p. 187.

[15] Grosart,I,349. Quoted in Geoffrey H. Hartman's *Wordsworth's Poetry, 1797-1814* (New Haven: Yale University Press, 1964), p. 278.

most part, absent from Wordsworth's late poems. Geoffrey Hartman's reference to the poet's "dignified self-consciousness" may suggest a less dynamic *self* than Coleridge was willing to accept. Coleridge's ultimate aim was to perfect self-love until it "annihilates Self, as a notion of diversity" (CN,III,4007), and Duty must resist the established forms of both Christianity and language so that it can promote self-evolution. Duty as an abstraction must be constantly rejuvenated, for Coleridge questioned "whether words as the already organized Materials of the higher Organic Life ... may not after a given period, become *effete?*"[16]

Coleridge's search for his "abstract self" led him to some happy collaborations with the physical world, to some poems in which he imagined an integrated self, fully at home in the world. To make of art "an image with a glory round its head" was to symbolize the Christian incarnation by marrying Thought and Thing. On the other hand, Duty was not always successful in compelling Coleridge to "Shine on!" Often juxtaposed to the integrated self in the same poem, we discover a self that cannot project onto nature, which becomes a *tabula rasa*, a desert, or the "blank lot and hard to bear." Doubt was essential to Coleridge's belief and he often had to imagine away the world's abundant consolations in order to discover inner Being. By imagining the universe as a "blank" he could, like Hegel, proceed to fill it. The dual functions of Coleridge's imagination, which could incorporate both positive and negative Being, helped him temper his belief. If we consider the complete notebook entry of "Coeli Enarrant" (CN,II,3107), rather than the last eleven lines that Ernest Hartley Coleridge chose to designate as the text (PW,I,486), we find that the poet alter-

---

[16] Alice D. Snyder, *Coleridge on Logic and Learning*, p. 138. Finding language itself "organic," Coleridge believed that a proper dictionary should be one that "regarding words as living growths, affects, and organs of the human soul, seeks to trace each historically through all the periods of its natural growth and accidental modifications" (p. 116). Coleridge's "organic form" is not simply a biological metaphor; a tree, a word, a self are all part of evolving life.

nates his two modes of thought: with Hope, nature is a self-reflecting mirror—I and World are "commensurate," harmonious—but when Coleridge's Hope becomes a lifeless abstraction, "Hopeless Hope," he is alone in the universe, forced to define himself against a meaningless backdrop. This "blank" becomes essential to his recognition of Being. As the poet wrote in his *Philosophical Lectures*: "if self-knowledge prevent this unmeaning blank, is not it a delightful, desirable object?" (PL,394).

Without the "undoubting Hope" found in its earlier section, "Coeli Enarrant" would appear to be a fragment of unalleviated despair, and some critics (I. A. Richards and James Boulger) have used the poem as evidence of Coleridge's loss of belief. But the beginning lines create a polarity within the total poem: Thought and Feeling can join in producing a harmonious state of bliss, past and future can be blended in "each sweet *now*." Coleridge's problem, however, is that even while imagining ecstasy, he feels compelled to wake from his dream and show that all natural life is without value if we see it only in terms of itself, without the "spectacles of faith." He celebrates the "life of the eye" in "Coeli Enarrant," but he also exposes the limitations of natural eyesight, as did Blake. We can learn to read the book of nature "aright" but the lesson is not easy, and like schoolchildren we may have to endure some strong discipline before we can discriminate between Phantom and Fact.


Fire, That slept in its Intensity, Life                    *f12*
Wakeful over all knew no gradations,
And Bliss in its excess became a Dream,
And my visual powers involved such Sense,
all Thought, Sense, Thought, & Feeling,
and Time drew out his subtle
Threads so quick, That the long
Summer's Eve was ~~long~~ one whole web,

A Space on which I lay commensurate—
For Memory & all undoubting Hope
Sang the same note & in the selfsame
Voice, with each sweet *now* of
My Felicity, and blended momently,
Like Milk that coming comes ~~of its steady~~ & in its
easy stream Flows ever in, upon the
mingling milk, in the Babe's murmuring
Mouth/or mirrors each reflecting each/—

———

Life wakeful over all knew no gradation
That Bliss in its excess became a Dream;
For every sense, each thought, & each sensation
Lived in my eye, transfigured ~~yet~~ not supprest.
And Time drew out his subtle threads so quick,
~~So softly too,~~ & And with such Spirit-speed & silentness,
That only in the web, of space like Time,
On the still spreading web I still diffused
Lay still commensurate—

———

What never is but only is to be
This is not Life—
O Hopeless Hope, and Death's Hypocrisy!
And with perpetual Promise, breaks its Promises.—

The Stars that wont to start, as on a chase,
And twinkling insult on Heaven's darkened Face,
~~And~~ Like a ~~bold~~ conven'd Conspiracy of Spies
Wink at each other with confiding eyes,
Turn from the portent, all is blank on high,
No constellations alphabet the Sky—
The Heavens one large black Letter only shews,
And as a Child beneath its master's Blows
Shrills out at once its Task and its Affright,
The groaning world now learns to read aright,
And with its Voice of Voices cries out, O!

Eyesight was a pervasive metaphor for Coleridge, one around which many of his thoughts about Being could cluster. The "visual powers" that he speaks of in the early part of the poem involve more than simple eyesight. The poet's unifying vision joins Thought and Feeling, and the physical senses are not degraded, only seen in their limited function. They need to be "transfigured not supprest." Earlier Coleridge had written: "O! what a life of the eye! What a strange inscrutable essence!" And he went on to show that the eye can be merely a recorder of Phantom sense impressions or, like a blindman's eye, have a "life" that is temporarily eclipsed:

> Even for him it exists, it moves and stirs in its prison;
> Lives with a separate life, and 'Is it a Spirit?' he
>   murmers:
> 'Sure it has thoughts of its own, and to see is only its
>   language.'

(PW,I,305)

In promoting not the eye but the abstracted Life of the eye, Coleridge makes an analogy between sensory apprehension and language that suggests the limitations of both. As the Thought of Sara finally proved to be of greater value than her actual presence, so the Life of the eye outlives actual seeing. Like the soul, "Its *Being*—enigmatic as it must seem —is posterior to its *Existence*" (CN,III,3593). Much is lost when we are denied the satisfactions of the here and now, but much is gained when the inner light and life are projected beyond "dark fluxion" because, as the poem "Limbo" demonstrates, the possibility of ultimate Being is realized. The unity that Coleridge sought, the "one life," is celebrated in the early portion of "Coeli Enarrant": Being and Becoming are "blended momently," and the speaker finds a correspondence in nature but is not arrested by it. This unifying vision is all-encompassing: time and space, those concepts created by the limited understanding, are one; human memory, no longer a reminder of loss and alienation,

blends with Hope for the future and sings "the same note &
in the selfsame/ Voice. . ." The poet's secondary imagination, being "essentially vital," is the "Life" of this poem:
it is "wakeful over all" as it "dissolves, diffuses, dissipates,
in order to recreate" (BL,I,202). Coleridge ends his evocation of Unity of Being with a metaphor that captures the
dynamic marriage of permanence and change, of spiritual
stillness and ongoing life:

> On the still spreading web I still diffused
> Lay still commensurate—

As with the stars in the gloss to *The Ancient Mariner* that
"still sojourn, yet still move onward," the emphatic repetition of "still" indicates the paradox of Being that cannot be
explained by any theory of knowledge. By the grace of his
benign imagination, the poet momentarily experiences a
Being that does not need to evolve: Life knows "no gradation."

The sublimity of these early lines, perhaps because they
have mystical, trance-like overtones, is balanced in Coleridge's notebook by a darker vision produced by the restless
mind, which always questions the Phantom peace of the
world. The "darkened Face" of heaven paradoxically
changes into an illuminating teacher, since it compels man
to "read aright" the shifting appearances of nature and to
"turn" within himself for the only substantial light. Rather
than a record of Coleridge's severed communion with God,
the latter part of the poem resembles a dark night of the
soul, a necessary stage preceding illumination. Characteristically, Coleridge must question the efficacy of his own
vision. Separating himself (and his readers) from his own
comforting metaphors, he announces that "all is blank on
high," but negation is, as Bergson said, "only an attitude
taken by the mind toward an eventual affirmation."[17] That
Coleridge claims his poem to be an "imitation of Du Bartas,

[17] Henri Bergson, *Creative Evolution*, trans. Arthur Mitchell (New
York: Macmillan, 1944), p. 312.

as translated by our Sylvester," should further warn us that the poet may be employing his negative "blank on high"[18] as a theme and not as a direct revelation of his own spiritual state.

Coleridge frequently used negation as a means of furthering, and not of undermining, his knowledge of himself. After an epiphany, the poet renews his search for more than momentary bliss. What if his memory of the past and his Hope for the future fail to blend? What if one of the dual mirrors that define the self should be shattered (as we saw in "Work Without Hope")? What if nature should remain a "blank" or speak a language he cannot understand? What if language should prove so false that it "mocks the mind with its own metaphors"? Coleridge even questioned his own acts of imaginative representation because, being fictive, they are possible Phantoms:

> What never is but only is to be
> This is not Life—

Life could never be a heavenly reward for having endured existence, Coleridge felt, just as a moral could not be the reader's reward for sharing the Mariner's awful experience. Death may end existence but not Life, for Life is a continuum, according to Coleridge. When the sun is eclipsed and the guiding stars seem absent—or what is worse, secretive and subversive—we face a "portent" that cannot be understood because it is of our own making. The sun is still there, although hidden, and the stars still journey and sojourn, but the impatient speaker remains unaware of what Coleridge declared in his "Dejection: An Ode":

> I may not hope from outward forms to win
> The passion and the life, whose fountains are within.

Unlike the "portent" in *Revelation* that offers an open door,

[18] Darkness (black) combines with "blank" (from the French "blanc"). Both extremes indicate an absence of the diverting, colorful *appearances* of external nature.

a voice, and seven torches of fire to light the way, Coleridge's "portent" is a Phantom that offers no *way* to Being.
In order to "turn from that portent" we must repent,[19] turn
back to ourselves, and give up seeking *objective* meaning
for the life within. Perhaps Coleridge considered the darkness a sign of the inadequacy of natural theology, and the
lines which Shakespeare wrote for Cassius seem true for
Coleridge: the fault does not lie in our stars but in ourselves.

Nevertheless, as Coleridge often said, nature is the symbolic language of God, if we could only learn to read it
correctly, distinguishing the spirit from the letter:

> For all that meets the bodily sense I deem
> Symbolical, one mighty alphabet
> To infant minds; and we in this low world
> Placed with our backs to bright Reality,
> That we may learn with young unwounded ken
> The substance from its shadow.
>
> *The Destiny of Nations* (PW,1,132)

The infant mind, like the rustic in "Constancy to an Ideal
Object," must realize that God manifests himself through
phenomena, but that human understanding becomes mere
superstition when it seeks "foresight without knowledge or
reflection" (*Friend*,1,57). Reading earthly or heavenly signs
can jeopardize our self-realization if we do not seek the
meaning behind such phenomena, the "bright Reality" at
our backs. The skies in "Coeli Enarrant" do not even contain an alphabet, only "one large Black letter" that seems to
forebode disaster. As his cancelled lines indicate, Coleridge
was describing the effect of an eclipse of the sun and probably, by extension, was alluding to astrologers who claim
to know the meaning of unusual natural occurrences. If
Coleridge had been more true to his source and less true to

---

[19] Both "reflection" and "repentance" involve a "turning back."
In *Aids to Reflection*, Coleridge uses the Greek word for repentance,
*matanoia*.

himself, he could have used Du Bartas' image of Christ as a hopeful contrast to his one black Letter:

> He in his hand the sacred booke doth bear
> Of that close-claspèd final *Calendar*;
> Where, in *Red letters* (now with us frequented)
> The certaine Date of that *Great Day* is printed. . .[20]

However, Coleridge chooses not to anticipate the last judgment, but rather to present in "Coeli Enarrant" his own conflicting experiences of Being, without the comforting assurances of the Christian tradition. In the early section, he creates metaphors of harmonious Being, a unity of Thought and Sense, a Hope that is alive and singing. But experience could not sustain such bliss. As we have seen many times before, Coleridge endured the blankness of nature as well as his "blank on high." We recognize his own duality in a footnote added to "Constancy to an Ideal Object," in which he described the extremes of his own visionary power: "the beholder either recognises it as a projected form of his own Being, that moves before him with a Glory round its head, or recoils from it as a Spectre" (PW,I,456). The two sections of "Coeli Enarrant" epitomize Coleridge's conflicting selves: the Babe "mingling milk" becomes "a Child beneath its master's Blows"; and the "Transfigured" world becomes a "groaning world." Coleridge accepts his own duality, his Joy and Despair, and thereby enlarges the range of his Being. Like the Mariner, the poet presents *experience as knowledge*, and the conclusion of this poem shows that his knowledge was achieved by suffering the wrath of a God more like Jehovah than Christ.[21]

[20] Joshuah Sylvester, *The Complete Works of Joshuah Sylvester*, 2 vols. ed. Alexander B. Grosart (New York: AMS Press, 1957), I, 23.

[21] Coleridge's fear of living a life of mere abstraction led him to exclaim that life is not "a sort of *knowledge*: No! it is a form of *Being* . . ." (*Friend*,I,524).

Ernest Hartley Coleridge's speculative dating of "Coeli Enarrant" (?1830) has led to the further speculation that Coleridge suffered a loss of faith in later life. But if the poem had been written earlier (1807), as Kathleen Coburn believes, we must wonder whether a great spiritual crisis has not been read into the poem. The idea that "Coeli Enarrant" may be an indirect assertion of belief grows more clear if we look at a stanza from the earlier "Ode to the Departing Year" (1796), in which the poet draws a parallel between a heavenly portent (the lampads Seven and the Mystic Words of *Revelation*) and a world that groans under the blows of an Avenger who inhabits a "storm-black Heaven." Coleridge's inflated rhetoric does not disguise this confrontation between Nature and the God of Nature, between man and an avenging Master. Nor does the public nature of the Ode conceal Coleridge's yearning for a personal God, one who can only be found through pain, suffering, and self-denial (the emphasis here is my own):

'Thou in stormy *blackness* throning
 Love and uncreated Light,
By the *Earth's unsolaced groaning*,
 Seize thy terrors, Arm of might!
By Peace with proffer'd *insult* scared,
 Masked Hate and envying Scorn!
 By years of Havoc yet unborn!
And Hunger's bosom to the frost-winds bared!
 But chief by Afric's wrongs,
  Strange, horrible, and foul!
 By what deep guilt belongs
To the deaf Synod, 'full of gifts and lies!'
By Wealth's insensate laugh! by Torture's howl!
  Avenger, rise!
 For ever shall the thankless Island scowl,
 Her quiver full, and with unbroken bow?
Speak! from thy storm-*black Heaven* O speak aloud!
  And on the darkling foe

Open thine eyes of fire from some uncertain cloud!
   O dart the flash! O rise and deal the *blow!*
The Past to thee, to thee the Future *cries!*
    Hark! how wide Nature joins her *groans* below!
    Rise, God of Nature! rise.'

                                (PW,I,165)

The "proffer'd insult" here anticipates the "twinkling insult" of "Coeli Enarrant," and the Nature that "joins her groans" returns later as the "groaning world." If God would only act, man might achieve peace through adoration, but the skies remain black and silent, and the spectator in both poems learns that he cannot will God into existence. However, the poet imagines the light away so that "Love and uncreated Light" can come into being.[22] His negative abstraction overpowers the consolation of philosophy, the distractions of phenomena, and the evasions of metaphor. He has created a total absence that only Being can fill. Rather than the cry of a lost soul, "Coeli Enarrant" may be one step in Coleridge's steady movement toward his "unborrow'd Self."

The Old Man in "Limbo" is Coleridge's most striking embodiment of the Christian paradox: this man is blind yet he watches the skies for what "seems to gaze on him!" He makes no attempt to explain life; he simply lives—and waits. Thus, what Coleridge warns us against in "Coeli Enarrant" is, perhaps, astrology parading as science (as wisdom) and superstition replacing true religion. The poet's humility before the mystery of Being was surely reinforced by his reading in Sylvester's "Little Bartas":

    Too-busy-bold with Thee, Lord, they presume;
And to themselves Thine Office they assume,
Who, by Star-gazing, or ought else below,
Dare arrogate the Future to foreknow.

[22] First hand Coleridge had discovered that "emptiness & absence, silence, darkness . . . are as positive Vorstellungen as Light, Sound, Image" (CN,II,3217).

> Wee hardly see what hangeth at our Eyes:
> How should wee read the Secrets of the Skies?[23]

When the sky is blank and the stars seem to conspire against us, we may learn to "read aright" by reflecting on ourselves, turning inward for the *"seeing* light" and the *"enlightening* eye" (AR,5). The world is not, in the end, a worthy object for our contemplation, and man is as unlikely to find himself reflected in the stars as he is to discover himself in a "narcissus pool" on earth. Coleridge wrote in another context: "the classical reader will recollect the image in Lucretius of Superstition looking down from the dark heaven," but his editor notes that in Lucretius "religion" is the figure looking down (ShC,1,73). Coleridge's misreading is very revealing, since from his early days he was preoccupied with the danger of confusing idols with religion, and visual representation with substantial truth. In his "Allegoric Vision" (PW,II,1091-1096), Superstition disguised as true religion offers some signs to the pilgrim who is lost in "perennial night":

> . . . a number of self-luminous inscriptions in letters of
> a pale sepulchral light, which held strange neutrality
> with the darkness, on the verge of which it kept its
> rayless vigil. I could read them, methought; but though
> each of the words taken separately I seemed to under-
> stand, yet when I took them as sentences, they were
> riddles and incomprehensible.

Unsatisfied by these "mysteries," the pilgrim at last encounters true religion, who provides him the proper means of seeing and enables him at last to encounter Being. As with the Brocken-Spectre metaphor, the world is neither explained nor transcended, but transfigured:

> She then gave us an optic glass which assisted without
> contradicting our natural vision, and enabled us to see
> far beyond the limits of the Valley of Life; though

[23] Sylvester, *Complete Works*, II, 88.

our eye even thus assisted permitted us only to behold
a light and a glory, but what we could not descry, save
only that it was, and that it was most glorious.

We do not see the object ("what") but we do apprehend
Being ("it was"). Whether they be stars or mountains, external things are incomprehensible riddles unless we abstract
ourselves from them and live with the paradox of "translucence":

> One lifts up one's eyes to Heaven as if to seek
there what one had lost on Earth/Eyes—
> Whose Half-beholdings thro' unsteady tears
> Gave shape, hue, distance, to the inward Dream/
> (CN,III,3649)

Perhaps Coleridge meant to indicate by that single Black
Letter the Omega of the last judgment—that Black Letter
day when all shall be "blank on high" and "the sun and
moon shall be dark, and the stars shall withdraw their
shining" (Joel 2:10). But, as we have seen, Coleridge was
unwilling to defer either negative or positive Being:

> What never is but only is to be
> This is not Life—

Though we cannot read meaning into the universe, we may,
like the Mariner, declare it, and to "read aright" means to
accept our "half-beholdings" and the "blank" we cannot
explain. After his isolation and suffering, the Mariner ex-
claims "O happy living things!" and we realize that he has
for the moment found meaning, the luxury of Being that
his suffering has earned. But in "Coeli Enarrant" the voice
that "cries out, O!" evokes the Christian passion, being half
joy, and half agony, the unresolved paradox of Being. The
pain of dying to the world precedes enlightenment. Once,
observing a halo around the moon, Coleridge wrote: "O!
it is a circle of Hope" (AP,283) But in "Coeli Enarrant" his
abstraction is without feeling, "O Hopeless Hope," and the

"one large black letter" in the sky, the eclipsed sun, signifies the world without God's presence. The poet had found the riddling "O" of existence even closer at hand: "in a single drop of water the microscope discovers, what motions, what tumult, what wars, what pursuits, what stratagems, what a circle-dance of Death & Life, Death hunting Life & Life renewed & invigorated by Death—the whole world seems here, in a many-meaning cypher—What if our existence was but that moment!—What an unintelligible affrightful Riddle" (CN,III,4057).[24] At the end of "Coeli Enarrant," the groaning world registers its "Affright" before existence, but it also realizes its "Task" which is to accept the struggle for Being, "by encroach of darkness made" (PW,I,394).

For Wordsworth, the stars represent a controlling order —a guide for mariners—and he never finds it necessary to imagine them away:

> Look for the stars, you'll say that there are none;
> Look up a second time, and, one by one,
> You mark them twinkling out with silvery light,
> And wonder how they could evade the sight![25]

But Coleridge needed to lose his way before he could find it, and like the Prodigal son he had to suffer alienation before he could discover Being. The complete notebook form of "Coeli Enarrant" resembles the pattern of Christian history. From a harmonious vision of Being the speaker falls into an alien world in which existence and Being are different, the past and future dissociated. By isolating man from society, Wordsworth hoped to reconcile man to nature and thereby to himself. But for Coleridge, this intermediary often failed to satisfy his profound spiritual hunger, as in these words he translated from Jean Paul: "we all look up to

---

[24] Coleridge's struggle might be indicated by the terms "riddle" and "paradox." He feared the riddle, with its meaning withheld, but he came to accept the paradox, which contains its meaning.

[25] "Evening Voluntaries I," *The Poetical Works of William Wordsworth*, IV, I.

the blue Sky for comfort, but nothing appears there—nothing comforts nothing answers us—& so we die" (CN,III, 4294). Mere eyesight apprehends only phantoms, counterfeits of the self, and the poet turns inward for the only true "portent": man's own prophetic soul. The object for man's contemplation is finally abstract, and through meditation he can approach "a bodiless Substance, an unborrow'd Self" (CN,II,2921). By abstracting himself from unthinking nature, the poet can begin "thinking himself"[26] and welcome the vacancy that makes Being possible:

> It is Night, sacred Night! The upraised Eye views only the starry heaven which manifests only itself—and the outward Look gazes on the sparks, twinkling in the awful Depth, to preserve the Soul steady and cocentered in its Trance of inward adoration.[27]

The poet's "Coeli Enarrant" showed that it was futile, perhaps even blasphemous, to try to interpret nature's signs, and to "read aright" seems to mean that we should give up fabricating explanations for objects—whether phenomena or what he called the "Phenomenon Self"—and strive to accept man as a subject capable of evolving an "Abstract Self." More and more in his later years, Coleridge reiterated that "There must be Reflection—a turning in of the Mind on itself. In order to be a Subject, the conscious Percipient and Appropriator of outward Objects, it must have been made itself an Object for itself—for so only can it know itself to be a *Subject* relatively to all else" (CL,V,517). Superstition, not true religion, presented the despairing sign

---

[26] "From the moment when Evolution begins to *think itself* it can no longer live with or further itself except by knowing itself to be irreversible—that is to say, immortal. For what point can there be in living with eyes fixed constantly and laboriously upon the future, if this future . . . must finally become a Zero? Better surely to give up and die at once." Pierre Teilhard de Chardin, *The Future of Man*, p. 206.

[27] Coleridge's marginal note to *Works of Jacob Behman* (London: 1761-81), I (1817), p. 47.

in the sky, and the poet repented and turned away, to seek Being through rigorous self-reflection. The short poem "Self-Knowledge," written in Coleridge's penultimate year, exposes the futile workings of the human "Understanding," which cannot solve the riddle of existence. The oracle at Delphi, which neither speaks nor conceals but gives signs, provides the epigraph for Coleridge's poem: "From Heaven descend: *Know Thyself*."

### Self-Knowledge

—E coelo descendit γνῶθι σεαυτόν [Know Thyself].
—Juvenal, xi,27.

γνῶθι σεαυτόν!—and is this the prime
And heaven-sprung adage of the olden time!—
Say, canst thou make thyself?—Learn first that trade;—
Haply thou mayst know what thyself had made.
What hast thou, Man, that thou dar'st call thine own?—
What is there in thee, Man, that can be known?—
Dark fluxion, all unfixable by thought,
A phantom dim of past and future wrought,
Vain sister of the worm,—life, death, soul, clod—
Ignore thyself, and strive to know thy God!

(PW,I,487)

The human Understanding has to be outgrown, since its very function is to deal with man in relation to external nature, and it inevitably ends up, as in Coleridge's poem "Human Life," viewing him only as a "Surplus of Nature's dread activity." Any object as an object was to Coleridge "dead, fixed, incapable in itself of any action, and necessarily finite" (BL,I,185). Although he had mirrored the "tragic dance" of life and death, the riddle of existence, in his poems, he had resisted efforts to "fix" his Being in time and space—or within a poem.

The directive provided by the adage "know thyself" is one more platitude, consisting of words that are meaningless until the poet tests their validity within his own life.

As in "Human Life," Coleridge gives the Understanding free rein so that it can expose its own inadequacy. We follow, as if steadily downward, a series of questions by which the speaker negates the human will, until man becomes only a series of nominatives without a verb that would signify his power to act: dark fluxion, a phantom, a sister of the worm, life, death, soul, clod. The lack of any syntactic action for the clustered names, and the rhetorical questions that seek no response, suggests that man's Reason has been trapped and, ironically, fixed by thought, the "stagnant understanding" (BL,I,169). Coleridge has brought degraded man to his nadir, a despair in which he seems *identified* with his material world. However, in the final injunction, the poet offers his own strong imperatives—"ignore" and "strive"—that urge man to pursue genuine abstraction. Coleridge wrote that the Mind is "a Subject including its Object," but it is also a "Verb," and united with the human will, it is a "Verb substantive" (CN,III,4412). At the end, the Understanding with its mere abstractions is rejected, and the poet affirms the active life of knowing, as contrasted with having what we commonly call the "body" of knowledge.

To "strive to know" God is very different from "to know" Him. In the act of writing his poem, Coleridge has reformed his title: self-knowledge, the phenomenal self as object, has become self-knowing, the self as a subject moving freely in its evolution toward God, "in whom we live and move and have our Being." One must ignore what is outside—ignore suggesting a willed act of rejection—in order to return to it, conscious of its true value. Because the external world is only a "modification of our own Being," man would be foolish to attempt to find there "the originals of the forms presented to him in his own intellect . . . [and] he learns at last what he *seeks* he had *left behind*, and but lengthens the distance as he prolongs the search" (*Friend*,I,509). The *already made* is a source of Phantom knowledge, thus the "trade" of making oneself, like Yeats's "sedentary trade" of poetry, produces uncertain results. In this world, meaning too frequently comes after the experience it would illuminate, and Coleridge admits the temporal restrictions that prevent many from self-knowledge: "*Haply* thou *mayst* know what thyself *had* made." To know only what *had* been made (*natura naturata*) is to know phenomenal man whose limited understanding associates him with his own past and not with abstract laws that govern the life of things. Reason is continually making the self, not trying to fix it *in* thought but to free it through thinking, and "true Being is Reason" (*Friend*,1,515,n2). As Dostoyevsky said, the only man whose mind is made up is a dead man.

Failing to see how Coleridge uses Reason to unmask the Understanding, some critics find pessimism in "Self-Knowledge," and other of his late poems. I. A. Richards, for example, asserts that Coleridge's lines "seem almost to spit scorn on the endeavour" of self-knowledge.[28] But, as we have seen before, Coleridge is presenting to us a productive paradox, not a sterile contradiction, and even though he is unable to resolve his own oppositions ("life, death, soul, clod") his poem does not end in "dark fluxion" but forcefully points toward the "knowledge that passeth all understanding." The poet's opposing selves (his Reason or positive Being, and his Understanding or negative Being) meet in the poem. Alienation becomes his means of forging a higher identity. The unaided understanding can only passively deduce a Phenomenal self, but by abstracting himself from phenomena the poet can will himself toward ideal Being: "to be known, this Identity must be dissolved—and yet it cannot be dissolved. For its Essence consists in this Identity. This Contradiction can be solved no otherwise, than by an Act, in consequence of which and from the necessity of Self-manifestation the Principle makes itself its own object, in and thus becomes a Subject,—The Self-affirmation is therefore

[28] I. A. Richards, *Coleridge on Imagination* (Bloomington: Indiana University Press, 1960), p. 50.

168

a Will: and Freedom is a primary Intuition, & can never be deduced" (CN,III,4265). Coleridge makes himself an object in a world of objects for the ultimate purpose of self-affirmation.

Because Richards believes that Coleridge's subject is his Self and his object is Nature, he reads "Self-Knowledge" as the poet's admission of defeat: nature no longer reflects the self. But rather than expressing "scorn, timidity and bafflement," the poem directly engages the problem of self-reflection: "the Christian world was for centuries divided into the Many, that did not think at all, and the Few who did nothing but *think*—both alike *unreflecting*, the one from defect of the *Act*, the other from the absence of the *Object*" (AR,184-85). By rejecting nature as an object, Coleridge freed himself to move beyond the self as an object until he could write "the I is not an Object; but a self-affirmed act" (CN,III,4356). The words "ignore thyself" are, as Richards rightly points out, uncharacteristic of Coleridge at any time in his earlier career, but they are also inapplicable to his later career unless we realize that the "self" has been divided. What Coleridge ignored throughout "Self-Knowledge" was, in Blake's term, his Spectre, his phenomenal self that, linked with matter, had to be left behind like a discarded evolutionary stage. By distinguishing two selves, Phenomenal and Abstract, Coleridge could define "The Duty Surviving Self-Love," which is to will our own spiritual evolution. To "ignore" the self as an object became a necessity, but to ignore the self as a subject would partake of that ignorance which is death.

The several references to "Know Thyself" that appear in Coleridge's writing indicate that he never abandoned his belief in knowledge of the abstract self as a correlative to knowing God. Although he recognized that "there is a strange—nay, rather a too natural—aversion in many to know themselves" (BL,II,212), he never avoided the agonizing choice that had to be made each time his own duality was exposed. Perhaps more than anything else, Coleridge feared self-contradiction, seeing it as characteristic of all pagan philosophies, and he advised man to "obey the simple unconditional commandment of eschewing every act that implies a self-contradiction" (*Friend*,I,150). As he demonstrated with heavy irony in his poem "Human Life," man cannot act and, incapable of self-reflection, cannot achieve even a momentary apprehension of Being: "Thy being's being is contradiction." The Mariner could not correct himself by means of thought, but he did risk his self by going to sea, and after an *act* of transgression he perhaps discovered that "the first step to knowledge, or rather the previous condition of all insight into truth, is to dare commune with our very and permanent self" (*Friend*,I,115). The loneliness of man when he lacks consoling earthly objects cannot be cured by the human understanding, which eventually turns in on itself and produces a self-circling form, an "eddy Without progression"—and one "recoils from the discovery" (*Friend*,I,509). But Coleridge leads his readers, as Virgil led Dante, downward toward despair until the inadequacy of the understanding has been proven, and the "scorn" that Richards detects is directed toward *one self only*. The other self is free to reason, to begin the painful process that is the birth and evolution of self-consciousness. The life of the reason is neither stagnant, nor self-circling, for it has a beginning, middle, and end—although the end of the "evolving line" cannot be revealed in human language except through paradox. Perhaps the simplest statement of this progressive realization of Being appears in the *Biographia Literaria*: "we begin with the *I* KNOW MYSELF, in order to end with the absolute *I* AM. We proceed from the SELF, in order to lose and find all self in GOD" (BL,I,186). The poet's creative acts serve this supreme end, as we know from Coleridge's definition of the primary imagination: "the living power and prime Agent of all human Perception, and as a repetition in the finite mind of the eternal act of creation in the infinite I am." For Coleridge, knowledge, abstract or otherwise, was always subordinate to Being and, like a modern existentialist, he asserted that "We must *be* it in order to *know* it" (CL,IV,768).

Coleridge's concept of Being could be articulated as an idea, but the poet had a difficult time making his living experience conform to this abstraction. His local mind had local hungers and was not easily absorbed into the universal mind. Before he could live with the abstraction Love, he had to outgrow his desire for an earthly vessel for it, whether in human or external nature. He knew that isolation and alienation had characterized his own existence, but he could not believe, like Kierkegaard, that a solitary state was essential to mankind's spiritual evolution. Yet the poet would have agreed with the theologian that "the merely human interpretation of love can never get further than reciprocity: the lover is the beloved, and the beloved is the lover. Christianity teaches that such a love has not yet found its right object—God. A love-relationship is threefold: the lover, the beloved, the love: but the love is God."[29] Coleridge's continual search for self-defining metaphors in his later poems reveals the difficulty of accommodating the absolute in our temporal language. He knew in his mind the "one absolute Object" (CN,II,3148) he must seek, but he had also learned from experience that a terrible coldness comes about when love suffers "the absence of objects to reflect the rays." In "The Blossoming of the Solitary Date-Tree," perhaps the only poem to result from his stay in Malta, Coleridge struggles to outgrow his dependence on phenomena. Through its external form and its thematic concerns, the poem both denies the possibility of fulfillment in the world and questions why this should be so.

The Blossoming of the Solitary Date-Tree
A Lament

I

BENEATH the blaze of a tropical sun the mountain peaks are the Thrones of Frost, through the absence of

[29] Kierkegaard, *Works of Love*, p. 99.

objects to reflect the rays. 'What no one with us shares, seems scarce our own.' The presence of a ONE,

The best belov'd, who loveth me the best,

is for the heart, what the supporting air from within is for the hollow globe with its suspended car. Deprive it of this, and all without, that would have buoyed it aloft even to the seat of the gods, becomes a burthen and crushes it into flatness.

### 2

The finer the sense for the beautiful and the lovely, and the fairer and lovelier the object presented to the sense; the more exquisite the individual's capacity of joy, and the more ample his means and opportunities of enjoyment, the more heavily will he feel the ache of solitariness, the more unsubstantial becomes the feast spread around him. What matters it, whether in fact the viands and the ministering graces are shadowy or real, to him who has not hand to grasp nor arms to embrace them?

### 3

Imagination; honourable aims;
Free commune with the choir that cannot die;
Science and song; delight in little things,
The buoyant child surviving in the man;
Fields, forests, ancient mountains, ocean, sky,
With all their voices—O dare I accuse
My earthly lot as guilty of my spleen,
Or call my destiny niggard! O no! no!
It is her largeness, and her overflow,
Which being incomplete, disquieteth me so!

### 4

For never touch of gladness stirs my heart,
But tim'rously beginning to rejoice
Like a blind Arab, that from sleep doth start
In lonesome tent, I listen for thy voice.

Belovéd! 'tis not thine; thou art not there!
Then melts the bubble into idle air,
And wishing without hope I restlessly despair.

5

The mother with anticipated glee
Smiles o'er the child, that, standing by her chair
And flatt'ning its round cheek upon her knee,
Looks up, and doth its rosy lips prepare
To mock the coming sounds. At that sweet sight
She hears her own voice with a new delight;
And if the babe perchance should lisp the notes aright,

6

Then is she tenfold gladder than before!
But should disease or chance the darling take,
What then avail those songs, which sweet of yore
Were only sweet for their sweet echo's sake?
Dear maid! no prattler at a mother's knee
Was e'er so dearly prized as I prized thee:
Why was I made for Love and Love denied to me?

(PW,I,396-97)

Beginning as prose (stanzas 1 and 2), the poem passes into
a stage of faltering poetry in which a rhyme scheme begins
to emerge (stanza 3), before assuming the formal regularity
of rhyme and meter in the last three stanzas. No single poem
of Coleridge's more forcefully demonstrates that the act of
making a poem was, for him, more important than the poem
itself, just as he comes to realize that the act of love does not
depend on anything but what is "within." It is not surpris-
ing, considering the poet's eclectic method, that the last
three stanzas may have been written long before the earlier
ones, and were arranged as a metaphor of evolving form, as
one critic believes.[30] In his prefatory note, Coleridge offers
this typically defensive evasion: the introductory stanzas

<hr>

[30] Max F. Schulz, *The Poetic Voices of Coleridge*, p. 159.

were once *complete* but are now missing, and "the author has in vain taxed his memory to repair the loss." Presenting to his reader a "rude draft," he invites him to collaborate in reconstructing a lost "object," and ends: "it is not impossible, that some congenial Spirit, whose years do not exceed those of the Author at the time the poem was written may find pleasure in restoring the Lament to its original integrity by a reduction of the thoughts to the requisite metre." The poet is apparently providing the *material* for a poem that the congenial reader must create. Again, Coleridge is indicating that Being is an act, a movement toward an ideal object.

Wordsworth could be happily alone with nature, and his choice of the "solitary" as the central metaphor for many of his poems suggests that the poet's "self" is secure, if not invulnerable, and is certainly not dependent upon other people. On the other hand, Coleridge's solitary figures in late poems like "The Blossoming of the Solitary Date-Tree" are painfully incomplete, and are either homesick or love-sick within an unreflecting landscape. In his earlier years, the poet's "seeming" could transform nature and he could enjoy the "luxury" of Being:

> It seem'd like Omnipresence! God, methought,
> Had built him there a Temple: the whole World
> Seem'd *imag'd* in its vast circumstance:
> No *wish* profan'd my overwhelméd heart.
> Blest hour! It was a luxury,—to be!
> "Reflections on Having Left
>   a Place of Retirement" (PW,I,107)

But even in youth, the delights of nature conceal a vacancy, an absent object that can give value to the physical scene:

> Ah! what a luxury of landscape meets
> My gaze! Proud towers, and Cots more dear to me,
> Elm-shadow'd Fields, and prospect-bounding Sea!
> Deep sighs my lonely heart: I drop the tear:
> Enchanting spot! O were my Sara here!
> "Lines" (PW,I,94)

Being in nature was a "luxury" that Coleridge could not long afford, and the title of Donald Wesling's essay on Wordsworth, *The Adequacy of Landscape*, would be appropriate for very few of Coleridge's poems.

In his fusing of man and nature in "Resolution and Independence," Wordsworth creates a physical "object" that he can read into, just as the Leech-Gatherer, in turn, can read in the "book" of nature.

> As a huge stone is sometimes seen to lie
> Couched on the bald top of an eminence;
> Wonder to all who do the same espy,
> By what means it could thither come, and whence;
> So that it seems a thing endued with sense:
> Like a sea-beast crawled forth, that on a shelf
> Of rock or sand reposeth, there to sun itself.

Wordsworth does not need to abstract himself from his experience of the natural world; by metaphoric extension he can unify man and thing without fear of becoming either a stone or a beast. In contrast, when Coleridge in 1819 said, "I would *allegorize* myself, as a Rock" (CL,IV, 975), he was lamenting his failure to find any fulfilling human relationship. To be isolated from human "otherness" was to be abandoned in nature, and his idea of Being was inextricably linked with the "other," whether it be Sara Hutchinson, his own "abstract self," or, finally, "the absolute I AM." Coleridge very early noted that "dear Wordsworth appears to me to have hurtfully segregated & isolated his Being" (CL,I,491), and the worst fate he imagined for himself was "to cocenter [his] Being into Stoniness, or to be diffused as among the winds, and lose all individual existence" (CL,II,1122). The Ancient Mariner's "loneliness and fixedness," unlike the Leech-Gatherer's, was seen as a mutation in the human evolutionary process; and when Coleridge recounted the "four griping and grasping Sorrows" of his whole life, he simply enumerated shattered love "objects": his alienation from his wife, his quarrel with Wordsworth, the loss of Sara Hutchinson, and his son Hartley's misspent life (CL,v, 249 ff). Since for Coleridge one must recognize Being in one's need for the "other," the solitary man is damned (the emphasis here is my own): "I *love* but few—but those *I love as my soul*—for I feel that without them I should —not indeed cease to be kind, and effluent; but—by little and little become a soul-less fixed Star, receiving no rays nor influences into my being, a solitude, which I so tremble at that I cannot attribute it even to the Divine Nature" (CL,v,240). The ultimate metaphor for this condition is the "Antipathist of Light" in "Ne Plus Ultra." Unlike Wordsworth's Solitary Reaper, Coleridge's solitary man neither reaps nor sings. Even though the poet understood as an artist that "the greater & perhaps nobler certainly all the subtler parts of one's nature, must be solitary—Man exists herein to himself & to God alone" (CN,i,1554), he remained unhappily in love with God.

Like many of Coleridge's poems, "The Blossoming of the Solitary Date-Tree" deals with severed communication, the loved one's silence portending an unresponsive God. Two metaphors that Coleridge used before, and will use again, reveal his need to find a Being that is not defined, hence limited, by his senses and sensory language: a blind Arab in the desert listening for a voice; and a parent (usually a mother) seeking the answering voice of a child. That these were metaphors for Being is made clear in a letter to Sotheby; "a great Poet must be, implicitè if not explicitè, a profound Metaphysician . . . he must have the *ear* of a wild Arab listening in the silent Desart, the eye of a North American Indian tracing the footsteps of an Enemy upon the Leaves that strew the Forest—: the *Touch* of a Blind Man feeling the face of a darling Child" (CL,ii,810). The poet and the metaphysician seek Being beyond nature's appearances, and neither echo nor mirror could satisfy Coleridge's need for original response, a need for the "other" that could complete his own self. The picture of a mother who is satisfied by an echo of her own voice is given a frightening variation in a simple notebook fragment that anticipated Coleridge's own spiritual desolation when earthly objects fail: "Mother listening for the *sound* of a still-born child—blind Arab list'ning in the wilderness" (CN,I,1244). Eventually, the *acts* of watching or listening, without any assurance of response, became his own expression of what we now call Christian Existentialism.

In "The Blossoming of the Solitary Date-Tree," Coleridge attempts to evade his very personal "ache of solitariness" by building a general context and telling his reader about "us" and "it" and "the individual's" capacity for joy. He tries to conceal his personal "ache of solitariness" within an "objective" discussion of the relationship of inner to outer world, of Phantom to fact, and he creates poetic analogies that are intended to make his problem less immediately personal. Coleridge witnessed one of the first hot air balloon ascensions and he may have brought that experience to his metaphor for the act of Being, which should not be restrained by the earth's gravity. However, the poet still laments the "absence of objects," even though he is striving to free himself of any dependence on them. In part three, he can still imagine "the buoyant child surviving in the man," but he cannot accept nature (or his "earthly lot") as an end for aspiring man because, despite its many voices, nature too lacks a counterpart:

> It is her largeness, and her overflow,
> Which being Incomplete, disquieteth me so!

The poet's analogies cannot long serve to distract him from his condition and the last three lines disrupt the decorum of the poem:

> Dear maid! no prattler at a mother's knee
> Was e'er so dearly prized as I prize thee:
> Why was I made for Love and Love denied to me?

177

Like Prufrock with his "overwhelming question," Coleridge acknowledges his own overwhelming need which neither art nor philosophy can fulfill. When years later Coleridge wrote to his friend Allsop about this poem, he recognized the duality he was struggling with, and also that he had not at the time (1805) succeeded in finding ideal objects to represent his abstractions Love and Hope: "*the man* in the Poet sighed forth" (CL,v,216). He had not achieved that union of subject and object that he called his "unborrow'd Self." Coleridge needed to imagine a transcendent "other" toward which he could direct his spiritual evolution. Sara Hutchinson was perhaps a synecdoche that for many years he imagined to be the whole. The Date-Tree, Coleridge said in a comment on the poem, bears fruit only when another of its kind is planted nearby. But the poet's parable, like the poem itself, must be read on an analogical level: "the yearning of the soul for its answering image and completing counterpart." The poet's "blossoming" bears fruit only as a higher consciousness.

In the very last year of his life, Coleridge returns to his solitary Arab in "Love's Apparition and Evanishment," but even though the figure is still passively attending some human voice, he performs an act of humility that seems to provide the answer to Coleridge's earlier self-pitying cry, "Why was I made for Love and Love denied to me?"

> And now he hangs his agéd head aslant,
> And listens for a human sound—in vain!
> And now the aid, which Heaven alone can grant,
> Upturns his eyeless face from Heaven to gain. . .

The Arab's gesture may indicate that Coleridge has found "a living instead of a reasoning Faith" (CL,III,462), and that he realizes that "Our misery may be a merciful mode of recalling us from our Self-chosen Exile" (CN,III,4341). Separated from a love object, Coleridge turned toward *the* love object, his own "Absolute" self, and ultimately toward the great "I AM."

Love's Apparition and Evanishment
An Allegoric Romance

Like a lone Arab, old and blind,
Some caravan had left behind,
Who sits beside a ruin'd well,
Where the shy sand-asps bask and swell;
And now he hangs his agéd head aslant,
And listens for a human sound—in vain!
And now the aid, which Heaven alone can grant,
Upturns his eyeless face from Heaven to gain;—
Even thus, in vacant mood, one sultry hour,
Resting my eye upon a drooping plant,
With brow low-bent, within my garden-bower,
I sate upon the couch of camomile;
And—whether 'twas a transient sleep, perchance,
Flitted across the idle brain, the while
I watch'd the sickly calm with aimless scope,
In my own heart; or that, indeed a trance,
Turn'd my eye inward—thee, O genial Hope,
Love's elder sister! thee did I behold,
Drest as a bridesmaid, but all pale and cold,
With roseless cheek, all pale and cold and dim,
    Lie lifeless at my feet!
And then came Love, a sylph in bridal trim,
    And stood beside my seat;
She bent, and kiss'd her sister's lips,
    As she was wont to do;—
Alas! 'twas but a chilling breath
Woke just enough of life in death
    To make Hope die anew.


L'Envoy

In vain we supplicate the Powers above;
There is no resurrection for the Love
That, nursed in tenderest care, yet fades away
In the chill'd heart by gradual self-decay.
                              (PW,I,488-89)

Called originally a madrigal and later an Allegoric Romance, "Love's Apparition and Evanishment" (1833-34) is composed of three parts: an extended metaphor, a personal account of a dream, and an "envoy" added after Coleridge's death, but written *and published* long before. The method is strikingly Coleridgean: three separate fragments are united to dramatize a spiritual condition, the poet's own accidie, the refusal of joy. The poet's uncertainty in naming his work is as characteristic as is his indifference to the sequence of its parts. The Envoy could serve equally as a prelude, as it does in what Ernest Hartley Coleridge calls the "first draft," and Coleridge's earlier editor was probably right when he says, "I doubt if these lines had originally any connection with the poem. They were composed on April 24, 1824."[31] In cases like this, Coleridge's conception of organic form seems questionable. How can these parts be said to "grow" when they are clearly assembled? Does not the poet contradict his own theory, as he also does in his marginal note to another poem: "these lines I hope to fuse into a more continuous flow, at least to articulate more organically"?[32] Because for some people "organic form" appears to sanction whatever comes *naturally* into the mind and onto the page, Coleridge's theory encounters considerable resistance.

Coleridge's favorite metaphor for his movement toward Being, a movement inherent in the process of making a poem, is that of a caterpillar evolving into a butterfly. Life precedes its outward manifestations, and parts of a poem may arrive from the unconscious mind at different times and be combined in different ways, as long as the life "within" is shaping the products. One need not create a new whole; one need only become more conscious of the kinship of parts, for "Whatever is grand, whatever is truly organic and living, the whole is prior to the parts" (PL,196). The process of creating a new consciousness of Being is

[31] James Dykes Campbell, *Poetical Works of Coleridge*, p. 645.
[32] Campbell, *Poetical Works of Coleridge*, p. 628.

difficult because the poet must overcome the strictures of sensory language, as the caterpillar strains to become a butterfly, freeing itself from Phantom appearance. If external nature is only "the *Mundus sensibilis*," then we can understand why there is something different from hubris in the poet's statement: "I can do what Nature per se cannot—I engraft" (CN,III,4060). The poet continues God's creation, as Florizel says Perdita does in *The Winter's Tale*: "what you do, still betters what is done." Both the spirits of nature and man are supersensuous but must act in order to keep from being identified with established forms, the already *made*, for "the Idea that puts the forms together, can not be itself form" (CN,III,4397). And for the poet, the dictionary meanings for abstractions like "Love" and "Hope" must be discarded like the "tegument that compressed the wings, and the antennæ of its [Psyche]" (CN,III,3362). Language must always be coming into Being in order to coincide with and express the poet's own life.

Coleridge's "Love's Apparition and Evanishment" is one last demonstration of the poet's negative Being in which he eddies without progressing and submits to the vacancy of outward forms. The passive, blind Arab who begins the "Romance" has been left behind in a lower state of development. Abandoned in nature, he still "Upturns his eyeless face," as does the Old Man in "Limbo," and thereby reveals his humility before the great "I AM." Hope is *in* his gesture, but it cannot assume its active life as an abstraction until the poet has, through his own will, "turn'd his eye inward." It seems necessary to be blind to the world, or blind to time and space like the poet in his "transient sleep" or "trance," before the abstractions "Love" and "Hope" can come to life. Coleridge recognized years earlier that he alone was responsible for his own peculiar development: "I seem to myself like a Butterfly who having foolishly torn or bedaubed his wings, is obliged to crawl like a Caterpillar with all the restless Instincts of the Butterfly" (CN,III,4088).

Like other of Coleridge's despairing poems, "Love's Ap-

parition and Evanishment" can be interpreted in the light
of the poet's theory of organic form: the poet considers a
stage of self-recognition that must be seen and abandoned
before any spiritual progress is possible. The Arab's blindness, like Coleridge's turning away from superficial metaphors, may be essential before the poet can restore life to
those stoney abstractions that were once fluid. The "sickly
calm," in which the poet can find no outlet *in nature*, may
be a necessary "disease," like Coleridge's sins, which he
viewed as painfully necessary to his evolution toward Being.
Unable to embody themselves in earthly objects, the abstractions "Love" and "Hope" continue their evolving life
within the consciousness. Hope, the awareness of possibility, seems dead; but Love, even though feeble and cold,
has the strength to induce Hope to reclaim some of its lost
power. In this drama of the mind, active Love refuses to
accept the Phantom appearance of death that she encounters
on Hope's face, so that the poet's marriage with his own
potentiality is still viable. Despite the pessimistic Envoy,
Love can always be resurrected if one moves away from
love of objects and toward love of Being itself. Phoenix-
like, Hope both lives and dies within an ongoing process
(not life or death, but life-in-death), so that, ironically, to
"die anew" is to be renewed, as in a Christian's daily death
to the world. That the poet's despair may be only temporary is implied in an early draft; the lines "There is no
resurrection for a love/ That uneclips'd, unshadowed, wanes
away" suggest that divine radiance is still present, if the poet
could but look beyond his earthly shadow. Coleridge could
not realize physical love for Sara Hutchinson in a physical
world, but he found that Love was still vital in the life of the
mind as an abstraction, although at times it was sadly a
"warmthless flame" (PW,I,457).

The "Allegory" of "Love's Apparition and Evanishment"
is not very clear, as Coleridge was well aware, and he wrote
in a letter that he someday hoped to improve the "*perspi-
cuity* in the Allegory" (CL,VI,952). But one doubts that he

cared to work very hard at spelling out a meaning separable from his dream experience. Just as he had moved away from metaphor, "a fragment of an allegory," he was no longer interested in perfecting a literary mode. He had imposed on himself the never-ending task of finding the word that could declare his own personal life; but as he progressed into the realm of abstraction, he knew that the task had become reversed: he must now discover the life in the word, whether it be Love or Hope or Youth. In the year of his death, Coleridge appeared nostalgic for "by-gone images" but he was also confident that he had come closer to "reality," to those "spice-islands of Youth and Hope, the two realities of this Phantom World. . . . I did not add Love: for this is only Youth and Hope embracing and so seen as *one*." Remaining true to his idea of spiritual evolution, he declared that reality is a "thing of Degrees" and that he had progressed toward it—"as far at least as Reality if predictable at all of aught below Heaven" (CL,VI,705).

"All 'genius' is now consumed. It could be of no further use, for it was only a means of attaining the final simplicity. There is no act of genius that is not *less* than the mere act of being."

Paul Valéry

"The sad ghost of Coleridge beckons to me from the shadows."

T. S. Eliot

# 5. Afterword:
## Journey of Two Magi

In "Journey of the Magi" T. S. Eliot creates a paradigm for his solitary struggle for Being that may help to illuminate Coleridge's similar experience, and may further suggest why both poets had difficulty accepting self-sufficient poetic forms to mirror their "desire beyond desire." Both desperately needed an absolute power to give meaning to the random fragments of living that some accept as life, but neither felt able to celebrate the Christian mystery without first evolving his own particular form that could incorporate both doubt and belief. At the same time, each needed to create a new self capable of living the Christian paradox of Being-in-Time. As Eliot wrote, with Johnsonian balance:

> It is not enough to understand what we ought to be, unless we know what we are; and we do not understand what we are, unless we know what we ought to be. The two forms of self-consciousness, knowing what we are and what we ought to be, must go together.[1]

They *must*. However, the failure of the human will to achieve such a consummation became the central concern of both Coleridge and Eliot. Prufrock's "scuttling" ends where it begins; the "fabulous junk" of *The Waste Land* (the phrase is Rose Macaulay's) promises only a possible redemption; the *Ash Wednesday* penitent fails to rise to divine union; and the speaker of the *Four Quartets* can only predict a time when "all shall be well." In "Journey of the Magi," the troubled Magus could be identified with both poets who have outgrown the physical world with its

[1] T. S. Eliot, "Religion and Literature," *Essays, Ancient and Modern*, p. 109.

images but lack the poetic magic to transport themselves
to a higher reality.

The structure of "Journey of the Magi" represents a
movement toward Being that cannot be completed and, like
one of Coleridge's eddies, must turn back upon itself. Temporal progress of life or a poem ends at the "frontiers of
consciousness"[2] where another kind of evolution begins.
The journey of this poem seems predicated on a goal that
can be realized, but it is one that must be self-*willed*. However, the temporal progress of the Magi seems governed by
vague impulse rather than motive, and the Magi seem almost
like automatons, passively "led." The early sections of the
poem describing the past journey are characterized by an
emphatic use of the co-ordinating conjunction "and," (with
two uses of "then"), that links events and images without
any controlling method, any subordination of one thing to
another, or any evaluation.[3] In the mind of the Magus things
happen fortuitously. They do not reveal Being to him; they
reveal only themselves. Recollecting the past, like Coleridge's Mariner, he reproduces rather than explains his experience, almost in the manner of free association (the
emphasis is mine):

> *And* the silken girls bringing sherbet.
> Then the camel men cursing *and* grumbling
> *And* running away, *and* wanting their liquor *and*
> women,
> *And* the night-fires going out, *and* the lack of shelters,
> *And* the cities hostile *and* the towns unfriendly
> *And* the villages dirty *and* charging high prices. . . .

[2] T. S. Eliot, "The Music of Poetry," *On Poetry and Poets* (New York: Noonday Press, 1961), p. 23. Coleridge uses a similar phrase, "the vestibule of Consciousness" (CL,ii,814). In turn, both call to mind Heidegger's "Threshold of Being."

[3] Almost a *tour de force*, the twenty-one uses of "and"/"then" in thirty-one lines suggest the relentless encroachment of a physical reality and a somewhat dispirited opposition to it: "and so we continued." One should note the contrasting use of "because" and "although" in *Ash-Wednesday*.

Because meaning is not inherent in the world, this series cannot be brought to any meaningful conclusion until its linear movement is disrupted, until the current running between man and a natural *telos* is short-circuited, sending energy inward (and eventually upward). To the human understanding, the voice that cries out "folly," the Nativity signifies only the physical poverty of the scene because transfiguration can take place only within the higher consciousness. When the Magus reaches his destination, he sings no hymn of praise, no "Joy to the World!" but appears unenthusiastic, if not disappointed:

> It was (you may say) satisfactory.

Rather than a failure of writing, as some suppose, Eliot's presentation of a less than joyful Incarnation is his means of exposing the counterfeit earthly end of this event and acknowledging his own incomplete faith. The word "satisfactory" suggests the presence of a grace that is sufficient but merely adequate, and further, may suggest a gratification of physical needs, "pleasure" rather than "joy." Eliot refrains from portraying the customary glorified reality in order to be true to his uncertain, individual *coming into Being*. Alienation from natural objects leads to alienation from the natural self; the inadequacies of "finite form" are revealed through Coleridge's "form that all informs against itself." Coleridge wrote that for men of genius "the love of the *means* is their end" (CN,III,3249), and many years after writing "Journey of the Magi," Eliot, referring to his own artistic journey in "East Coker," still sounds very much like his Magus:

> It was not (to start again) what one had expected.

After confronting the Christ child, the Magus returns to his old kingdom with its old dispensation. Separated from physical nature, from his own society and culture, even from the "We" of his group experience, he is alone in his Being, a solitary "I." And Like many of Coleridge's isolated

187

figures, he is in need of a regeneration that can only come from within:

> All this was a long time ago, I remember,
> And I would do it again, but set down
> This set down
> This: were we led all that way for
> Birth or Death? There was a Birth, certainly,
> We had evidence and no doubt. I had seen birth and
>   death,
> But had thought they were different; this Birth was
> Hard and bitter agony for us, like Death, our death.
> We returned to our places, these Kingdoms,
> But no longer at ease here, in the old dispensation,
> With an alien people clutching their gods.
> I should be glad of another death.

Temporarily fixed between two levels of consciousness, the Magus endures his time in Limbo, Coleridge's "intermundium," which Eliot in his own way describes as "the neutral territory/ Between two worlds" that is also a zone "between two lives."[4] Before he can discover the meaning he failed to recognize, the meaning that would have made his experience more than satisfactory, he must through self-reflection begin to create a new self, not one reflected from nature. He must lead and not be led. But the Magus is not yet capable of living in a paradox without trying to resolve it. That he is "no longer at ease" may perhaps indicate his greater spiritual "dis-ease," which now recognized he can begin to cure. Coleridge often associated disease with any change in an organism that preceded growth: "Dolor animæ se ipsam parturientis . . . the convulsive agonies of the Caterpillar in its laborious forth-struggle from the tegument that compressed the wings, and the antennæ of its $\psi v \chi \acute{\eta}$— ["soul" as well as "butterfly"]" (CN,III,3362). The Magus discovered not what he wanted but what he needed; he

---

[4] The "Twilight kingdom" is, of course, most notable in Eliot's "The Hollow Men."

continues to suffer the alienation that affects every mortal except the prophet, and that, for Eliot, became a dissociation that continually troubled him: "We had the experience but missed the meaning."

For both Coleridge and Eliot, paradox had to be the means of breaking the sequence of conceptual logic, as well as the straight line of history (an endless series of events connected by "ands"), and of freeing Being from its natural, confining form. The terms devised by the limited understanding to represent clear opposites (Life and Death) must be dislocated, and like all abstractions, be redefined not as mere concepts but within the individual life. The Mariner had seen the personified figures of Death and Life-in-Death on a ghost ship, but he had also seen Life in water-snakes: "O happy living things!" For Coleridge, Being quickens when opposites come together but are not annihilated. The words of Eliot's Sweeney in "Fragment of an Agon" could speak for both the Mariner and the Magus:

> When you're alone like he was alone
> You're either or neither
> I tell you again it dont apply
> Death or life or life or death
> Death is life and life is death
> I gotta use words when I talk to you. . . .

Being can only be declared through *apparent* contradiction because of the limitations of human language and human understanding. The human choice, however, must be not between the two extremes, but a choice to invoke the power of the verb "to be" that marries the two ("death is life").

The Magus' inability to find illumination in the external world (the "watermill beating the darkness" does not beat it into inner light) compels him to put his own mind to work, causing abstractions like Life and Death to discover their meaning within *a* life and *a* death. He had "seen birth and death,/ But had thought they were different," but now he begins to realize a truth that cannot be verified through

the senses: that Life and Death are one in Christ's Passion.[5]
Eliot's capitalization at the end of "Journey of the Magi"
may distinguish the abstract from the particular, the universal from the local mind. Despite his doubts and confusion,
the Magus does not despair: "I *would* do it again." But even
though he is committed to enduring the hardship of his
"cold coming" into Being, a contingency impinges on his
final assertion, "I *should* be glad of another death."[6] The
conditional tense once more attests to the difficulty of fixing
a spiritual condition in language that is itself only a means
to an end. Years later in "Little Gidding" Eliot could still
have been referring to the alienated Magus: "what you
thought you came for/ Is only a shell, a husk of meaning."
Moreover, this explanation also conveys a warning to readers of Coleridge's and Eliot's fragments. If a poem is a piece,
it must be a piece of something. The husk or shell testifies
to a life that has moved beyond the stages of phenomenal
form.[7] It seems as if Eliot could often have been speaking for
Coleridge as well as himself: "every poem an epitaph"
("Little Gidding"), and "the poetry does not matter" ("East
Coker").

Although Coleridge's journey toward Being seems to pos-

[5] "Know ye not that so many of us as were baptized into Jesus
Christ were baptized into his death? Therefore we are buried with
him by baptism into death" Romans, VI, 3-4.

[6] Even assuming British usage, "I should be glad of another death"
remains marked by a condition not explained. The lower case
"death" may indicate the Christian's need for daily death to the
world, but the line could also include the possibility of a suicidal
despair.

[7] Eliot's comment on "Kubla Khan" seems puzzling, considering
his own practice of shoring fragments against his ruin: "the imagery
of that fragment, certainly, whatever its origin in Coleridge's reading,
sank to the depths of Coleridge's feeling, was saturated, transformed
there—'those are pearls that were his eyes'—and brought up into
daylight again. But it is not *used*: the poem has not been written. . . .
Organization is necessary as well as 'inspiration!'" *The Uses of
Poetry and the Uses of Criticism* (London: Faber & Faber, 1933),
p. 146.

sess more spiritual energy than Eliot's, he nevertheless deals
with the same paradoxical reconciliation of opposites. Coleridge did experience moments charged with joy, even at
those times when he could imagine the power only for
another, as in his "Dejection: An Ode":

> Joy, Lady! is the spirit and the power,
> Which wedding Nature to us gives in dower
>   A new Earth and a new Heaven,
> Undreamt of by the sensual and the proud—
> Joy is the sweet voice, Joy the luminous cloud—
>   We in ourselves rejoice!

However, Coleridge, as often as Eliot, dealt with an opposing, negative power, the despair that Eliot said was "a necessary prelude to, and element in, the joy of faith."[8] In *The
Ancient Mariner* the word "joy" appears three times in the
later gloss; and like Kierkegaard's use of "joy" in his commentary on The Prodigal Son, the word involves *arrival*,
the coming together of experience and its transfiguring
meaning. The arrival of the albatross produces joy, as does
the arrival of the lordly stars, and the arrival of the ghost
ship creates what turns out to be a Phantom joy. But after
these moments, which can indicate the moments of positive
Being that Coleridge enjoyed in his lifetime, the Mariner
reaches shore—and no joy ensues. Despite the "hard and
bitter agony," neither the Magus nor the Mariner, neither
Coleridge nor Eliot, finally arrives. The journey always
continues in the mind, a life of paradox, as in "East Coker":

> We must be still and still moving
> Into another intensity
> For a further union, a deeper communion. . . .[9]

Coleridge's journey into "further union," his "ultimate

---

[8] T. S. Eliot, *Selected Essays*, p. 412.
[9] Coleridge anticipates Eliot's central paradox in the celebrated
moon gloss to *The Ancient Mariner*, in which stars "still sojourn,
yet still move onward."

Being," may continue beyond the "Epitaph" he created for himself that significantly appears in six differing versions.[10]

> Stop, Christian Passer-by!—Stop, child of God,
> And read with gentle breast. Beneath this sod
> A poet lies, or that which once seem'd he.
> O, lift one thought in prayer for S.T.C.;
> That he who many a year with toil of breath
> Found death in life, may here find life in death!
> Mercy for praise—to be forgiven for fame
> He ask'd, and hoped, through Christ. Do thou the same!
>
> (PW,I,491-92)

Uncertain about everything but his lifelong need for certainty, Coleridge records the earthly suffering that has brought him to an end that he hopes will be a beginning. He had written years earlier that Thought and Reality are "two distinct corresponding Sounds, of which no man can say positively which is the Voice and which the Echo" (CN,II,2557), and we find him again constructing such balances, but declaring that his Being rests in the coming together of opposites. He, like the Magus, has endured a life of abstraction without the consolation of metaphor, and he is left only with possibility. Has his life as a poet been a Phantom existence? Has he only "seem'd" to be a poet, just as the lifeless corpse below the gravestone is now an impersonal pronoun ("that") standing for a man who in turn stood for a poet?[11] It is the man and not the masquerading poet whom Coleridge wishes us to rescue from death through our "thought in prayer": not Samuel Taylor Coleridge, a name on books, but S.T.C., the unique, personal

[10] Typically evading genre designation, Coleridge calls one version "On a Tombstone" (CL,VI,963), another simply "S.T.C." (CL,VI,973). But the fact that he wanted the epitaph with its accompanying drawing to appear *in print* may again show his preference of the life of the mind over dead external forms.

[11] Coleridge's shift from "was" to "seem'd" reveals his continuing need to distinguish Being from its Phantom appearances.

signature of his authentic Being. Rejecting the figure of a muse that an artist had drawn for his tombstone, Coleridge wrote that he preferred a "hint of Landscape" and no mythical figure but "an elderly man, Thoughtful, with quiet tears upon his cheek" (CL,vi,968-69). It is in thought that his progress toward Being occurred, and so he asks the reader of his epitaph to provide the thought in which this evolution may continue. The Life-in-Death that appeared as a nightmare figure to the suffering Mariner is no longer an image but an abstraction, grounded in experience and not in an object or poem—the "toil of breath" suggesting the poet's articulations as well as the man's struggle for Being. Paradox remains the best means of confronting despair, and Coleridge accepts a past discovery ("Found death in life") that unites with a future possibility ("May here find life in death," a forgiveness that *is to be*). Having outgrown a need for objects of sense and their metaphoric representations, the poet attains a final simplicity. With neither pious resignation nor the tired indifference that only appears to be belief, Coleridge is still engaging the opposites that generated his life and art. The final reconciliation was not in his hands.

# Works Cited

Allsop, Thomas. *Letters, Conversations and Recollections of S. T. Coleridge.* 2 vols. London: Edward Moxon, 1836.

Barfield, Owen. *What Coleridge Thought.* Middletown, Conn.: Wesleyan University Press, 1971.

————. *Poetic Diction.* Middletown, Conn.: Wesleyan University Press, 1972.

Barth, J. Robert. *Coleridge and Christian Doctrine.* Cambridge, Mass.: Harvard University Press, 1969.

Bate, Walter Jackson. *Coleridge.* New York: Macmillan, 1968. Masters of World Literature Series.

Beer, John. *Coleridge's Poetic Intelligence.* New York: Harper & Row, 1977.

Blake, William. *The Poetry and Prose of William Blake.* Edited by David V. Erdman. New York: Doubleday Anchor Book, 1965.

Boulger, James. *Coleridge as Religious Thinker.* New Haven: Yale University Press, 1961.

Campbell, James Dykes. *The Poetical Works of Samuel Taylor Coleridge.* London: Macmillan, 1893.

Coburn, Kathleen. "Coleridge: A Bridge between Science and Poetry." *Coleridge's Variety: Bicentenary Studies.* Edited by John Beer. Pittsburgh: University of Pittsburgh Press, 1975.

Collingwood, R. G. *The Principles of Art.* New York: Oxford University Press, 1958.

Davie, Donald. *Articulate Energy.* London: Routledge & Kegan Paul, 1955.

Eliot, T. S. *The Complete Poems and Plays.* New York: Harcourt, Brace & Co., 1952.

————. Preface to *Anabasis.* New York: Harcourt, Brace & Co., 1949.

————. *Essays, Ancient and Modern.* London: Faber & Faber, 1936.

————. *On Poetry and Poets.* New York: Noonday Press, 1961.

Eliot, T. S. *The Uses of Poetry and the Uses of Criticism*. London: Faber & Faber, 1933.

Empson, William, and David Pirie, eds. *Coleridge's Verse: A Selection*. London: Faber & Faber, 1972.

Hartman, Geoffrey H. *Wordsworth's Poetry, 1797-1814*. New Haven: Yale University Press, 1964.

Heidegger, Martin. *On Time and Being*. Translated by Joan Stambaugh. New York: Harper & Row, 1972.

———. *Being and Time*. Translated by John Macquarrie and Edward Robinson. New York: Harper & Row, 1962.

———. *Poetry, Language, Thought*. Translated by Albert Hofstadter. New York: Harper & Row, 1971.

Herbert, George. *Works*. Edited by F. E. Hutchinson. Oxford: Clarendon Press, 1945.

House, Humphrey. *Coleridge: The Clark Lectures, 1951-52*. London: Rupert Hart-Davis, 1953.

Jackson, J. R. de J., ed. *Coleridge: The Critical Heritage*. London: Routledge & Kegan Paul, 1970.

Jones, John. *The Egotistical Sublime: A History of Wordsworth's Imagination*. London: Chatto & Windus, 1954.

Kenner, Hugh. *The Pound Era*. Berkeley and Los Angeles: University of California Press, 1971.

Kierkegaard, Søren. *Concluding Unscientific Postscript*. Translated by David F. Swenson and Walter Lowrie. London: Oxford University Press, 1941.

———. *Works of Love*. Translated by David F. Swenson and Lillian Marvin Swenson. London: Oxford University Press, 1946.

Laing, R. D. *The Divided Self*. London: Penguin Books Ltd., 1965. Pelican Edition.

McFarland, Thomas. *Coleridge and the Pantheist Tradition*. Oxford: Clarendon Press, 1969.

Perkins, David. *The Quest for Permanence*. Cambridge, Mass.: Harvard University Press, 1969.

Potter, Stephen. *Coleridge and S. T. C.* London: Jonathan Cape, 1935.

———. *Coleridge: Selected Poetry and Prose*. London: Nonesuch Press, 1933.

Prickett, Stephen. *Coleridge and Wordsworth: The Poetry of Growth*. Cambridge: Cambridge University Press, 1970.

Read, Herbert. *The True Voice of Feeling: Studies in English Romantic Poetry*. London: Faber & Faber, 1938.

Richards, I. A. *Coleridge on Imagination*. Bloomington: Indiana University Press, 1960.

Schulz, Max F. *The Poetic Voices of Coleridge*. Detroit: Wayne State University Press, 1964.

Snyder, Alice D. *Coleridge on Logic and Learning*. New Haven, Conn.: Yale University Press, 1929.

Summers, Joseph H. *George Herbert: His Religion and Art*. Cambridge, Mass.: Harvard University Press, 1954.

Sylvester, Joshuah. *The Complete Works of Joshuah Sylvester*. 2 vols. Edited by Alexander B. Grosart. New York: AMS Press, 1957.

Taylor, Jeremy. *Polemical Discourses*. London, 1674.

Teilhard de Chardin, Pierre. *Christianity and Evolution*. New York: Harcourt Brace Jovanovich, 1969.

———. *The Future of Man*. London: Collins, 1964.

Valéry, Paul. *The Art of Poetry*. Translated by Denise Folliot. New York: Pantheon Books, 1958.

———. *Leonardo, Poe, Mallarmé*. Translated by Malcolm Cowley and James R. Lawler. Princeton, N.J.: Princeton University Press, 1972.

Vendler, Helen. *The Poetry of George Herbert*. Cambridge, Mass.: Harvard University Press, 1975.

Walsh, William. *Coleridge: The Work and the Relevance*. London: Chatto & Windus, 1967.

Watson, George. *Coleridge the Poet*. London: Routledge & Kegan Paul, 1966.

Wesling, Donald. *Wordsworth and the Adequacy of Landscape*. New York: Barnes & Noble, 1970.

Whalley, George. *Coleridge and Sara Hutchinson and the Asra Poems*. London: Routledge & Kegan Paul, 1955.

Willey, Basil. *Samuel Taylor Coleridge*. New York: W. W. Norton & Co., 1973.

# Index of Names

Allsop, Thomas, 116, 178

Barfield, Owen, 55, 73, 115, 123, 130
Barth, J. Robert, 91, 110
Bate, Walter Jackson, 5
Beer, John, 16, 148
Behman, Jacob, 165
Berengarius of Tours, 92, 94, 107
Bergson, Henri, 156
Berkeley, George, 133
Blake, William, 29, 31, 43, 61, 73, 105, 107, 110, 131, 141, 148, 153, 169
Boulger, James, 70, 71, 153

Campbell, James Dykes, 84, 114, 180
Coburn, Kathleen, 114, 118, 148, 160
Coleridge, Derwent, 17, 28
Coleridge, Ernest Hartley, 114, 117, 118, 152, 160, 180
Coleridge, Hartley, 27, 28, 99, 176
Collingwood, R. G., 49
Cowper, William, 126

Dante Alighieri, 43, 44, 45, 170
Davie, Donald, 49
Dostoyevsky, Feodor, 168
Du Bartas, Guillaume de Saluste, 156, 159, 161

Eliot, T. S., 68-69, 71-72, 84-85, 100, 101, 103, 116, 132, 138, 141, 178, 184, 185-193
Empson, William, 71
Erdman, David V., 29, 31

Fenollosa, Ernest, 124
Frost, Robert, 20
Fuller, Thomas, 91

Gillman, James, 116
Grosart, Alexander B., 159

Hartley, David, 133
Hartman, Geoffrey H., 151, 152
Hazlitt, William, 4
Hegel, Georg Wilhelm Friedrich, 152
Heidegger, Martin, 6, 7, 12, 186
Herbert, George, 76-78, 80, 91, 93, 100, 125
Hopkins, Gerard Manley, 46
House, Humphrey, 60, 114
Hughes, Joseph, 103
Hulme, T. E., 124
Hutchinson, Sara, 15, 16, 18, 31, 32, 33, 36, 41, 42, 44, 45, 47, 50, 51, 61, 86, 94, 103, 111, 112, 123, 126, 131, 132, 133, 135, 139, 143, 144, 145, 146, 147, 150, 155, 175, 176, 178, 182

199

Jackson, J. R. de J., 4
Jones, John, 151

Keats, John, 17, 56, 64, 99, 126, 132
Kenner, Hugh, 15
Kierkegaard, Søren, 54, 74, 88, 146, 171, 191

Laing, R. D., 77

Macaulay, Rose, 185
McFarland, Thomas, 68
Milton, John, 36, 91, 99, 107
Moore, Henry, 90

Newton, Isaac, 43

Paul, Jean, 164
Perkins, David, 139
Pirie, David, 71
Potter, Stephen, 20, 23, 36
Pound, Ezra, 15, 124-125
Prickett, Stephen, 127

Read, Herbert, 125
Richards, I. A., 153, 168, 170
Rousseau, Jean Jacques, 94

Schelling, Friedrich Wilhelm Joseph von, 132
Schlegel, August Wilhelm von, 22

Schulz, Max F., 48, 173
Shakespeare, William, 10, 23, 28, 30, 79, 93, 134, 136, 137, 158, 181
Shedd, W.G.T., 68, 71, 133
Sidney, Sir Philip, 125
Snyder, Alice D., 14, 86, 125, 152
Southey, Robert, 18, 110
Spenser, Edmund, 125
Summers, Joseph H., 80
Sylvester, Joshuah, 157, 159, 161, 162

Taylor, Jeremy, 110
Teilhard de Chardin, Pierre, 30, 165
Tuve, Rosemond, 78

Valéry, Paul, 16, 118, 184
Vendler, Helen, 78

Walsh, William, 127
Watson, George, 70, 113
Wesling, Donald, 175
Whalley, George, 84
Willey, Basil, 4
Wordsworth, William, 3, 17, 20, 24, 25, 26, 27, 47, 57, 64, 72, 91, 94, 110, 134, 138, 139, 147, 148, 149, 150, 151, 164, 174, 175, 176

Yeats, William Butler, 102, 168

# Index of Works by Coleridge

*Aids to Reflection*, 4, 11, 14, 17, 25, 31, 35, 39, 41, 42, 45, 48, 54, 55, 65, 66, 73, 90, 107, 128, 134-135, 158, 162, 169
"Allegoric Vision," 101, 162
*Anima Poetae*, 20, 30, 147, 163
"Apologia Pro Vita Sua," 39, 45, 128

*Biographia Literaria*, 7, 8, 21, 25, 74, 75, 79, 92, 102, 108, 111, 112, 127, 131, 132, 134, 149, 156, 166, 167, 169, 170
"Blossoming of the Solitary Date-Tree, The," 5, 171-178

"Coeli Enarrant," 152-165
*Collected Coleridge, The*, 12
*Confessions of an Inquiring Spirit*, 91
"Constancy to an Ideal Object," 62, 127-137, 139, 158, 159

"Dejection: An Ode," 11, 15, 18, 31, 32, 33, 34, 35, 36, 51, 57, 86, 103, 104, 109, 124, 145, 157, 191
"Destiny of Nations, The," 22, 158
"Duty Surviving Self-Love," 5, 147-152, 169

"Eddy-Rose, The," 12, 18, 19, 21, 22, 24, 28, 34
"Epitaph," 192-193

*Fall of Robespierre, The*, 125
"Fancy in Nubibus," 94
"Fears in Solitude," 126
*Friend, The*, 5, 21, 27, 38, 55, 57, 59, 71, 74, 88, 94, 101, 104, 105, 108, 113, 114, 116, 123, 124, 134, 137, 144, 158, 159, 167, 168, 170
"Frost at Midnight," 17, 20, 21, 31, 35, 41, 51, 65, 108, 136

"Hexameters," 155
"Human Life," 69-80, 167, 170

"Improvisatore, The," 8, 88, 119

"Kubla Khan," 21, 24, 35, 59, 60, 61, 190

*Lay Sermons*, 29, 87
*Letters, Coleridge's Collected*, 3, 4, 7, 9, 10, 11, 13, 15, 24, 28, 30, 33, 36, 37, 39, 44, 46, 50, 54, 59, 61, 64, 65, 67, 71, 75, 76, 87, 90, 91, 93, 94, 99, 100, 106, 107, 108, 115, 116, 120, 123, 124, 127, 131, 134, 138, 140, 142, 143, 144, 147, 149, 151, 165, 171, 175, 176, 178, 182, 183, 186, 192, 193
"Limbo," 3, 7, 12, 83, 90-120, 123, 133, 138, 155, 161, 181
"Lines . . . Berengarius," 92, 94
"Lines . . . Brockley Coomb," 174

*Literary Remains*, 8, 12, 36, 51, 74, 80, 83, 90, 91, 100, 102, 107, 110

"Love's Apparition and Evanishment," 178-183

*Miscellaneous Criticism*, 28, 48, 59, 90, 91, 109, 147

"Ne Plus Ultra," 93, 104, 111-113, 118-119, 176

"Night-Scene, The," 34

*Notebooks, Collected*, 9, 10, 12, 16, 17, 19, 24, 26, 27, 32, 34, 35, 36, 37, 39, 40, 41, 42, 43, 46, 47, 49, 51, 58, 59, 60, 71, 72, 76, 82, 84, 85, 86, 89, 90, 100, 104, 109, 111, 112, 120, 122, 123, 128, 131, 135, 136, 137, 142, 145, 146, 147, 150, 151, 152, 155, 161, 163, 164, 165, 167, 171, 176, 177, 178, 181, 187, 192

"Ode to the Departing Year," 58, 160

"On Donne's first Poem," 114, 115

"Orpheus," 25-26, 27

"Phantom," 6, 40, 41, 42, 43, 44, 45, 46, 47, 49, 51, 53, 55, 58, 61, 94, 128, 132, 145

"Phantom or Fact," 5, 51, 52, 53, 54, 55, 56, 61, 66

*Philosophical Lectures*, 23, 70, 72, 74, 89, 104, 113, 117, 137, 143, 144, 153, 180

"Picture, The," 61-68, 74

"Reason," 43-44

"Reflections on Having Left a Place of Retirement," 126, 174

*Remorse*, 58

"Rime of the Ancient Mariner, The," 7, 22, 30, 48, 49, 53, 85, 100, 105, 106, 130, 132, 147, 156, 157, 159, 163, 170, 175, 186, 189, 191, 193

"Self-Knowledge," 166-171

*Shakespearean Criticism*, 23, 57, 78, 90, 99, 115, 116, 118, 137, 139, 146, 162

*Sibylline Leaves*, 70, 84

*Statesman's Manual, The*, 30, 43

*Table Talk*, 24, 54

*Theory of Life*, 45, 72, 107

"Time, Real and Imaginary," 83-90

"To William Wordsworth," 25

"Tombless Epitaph, A," 68

*Treatise on Method*, 12, 22, 38, 134

"Two Founts, The," 23

"What is Life?," 59

"Work Without Hope," 79, 138, 139-144, 157

"Youth and Age," 5, 76, 88-89

# Princeton Essays in Literature

*The Orbit of Thomas Mann.* By Erich Kahler

*On Four Modern Humanists: Hofmannsthal, Gundolf, Curtius, Kantorowicz.* Edited by Arthur R. Evans, Jr.

*Flaubert and Joyce: The Rite of Fiction.* By Richard Cross

*A Stage for Poets: Studies in the Theatre of Hugo and Musset.* By Charles Affron

*Hofmannsthal's Novel "Andreas."* By David H. Miles

*Kazantzakis and the Linguistic Revolution in Greek Literature.* By Peter Bien

*Modern Greek Writers.* Edited by Edmund Keeley and Peter Bien

*On Gide's Prométhée: Private Myth and Public Mystification.* By Kurt Weinberg

*The Inner Theatre of Recent French Poetry.* By Mary Ann Caws

*Wallace Stevens and the Symbolist Imagination.* By Michel Benamou

*Cervantes' Christian Romance: A Study of "Persiles y Sigismunda."* By Alban K. Forcione

*The Prison-House of Language: a Critical Account of Structuralism and Formalism.* By Frederic Jameson

*Ezra Pound and the Troubadour Tradition.* By Stuart Y. McDougal

*Wallace Stevens: Imagination and Faith.* By Adalaide K. Morris

*On the Art of Medieval Arabic Literature.* By Andras Hamori

*The Poetic World of Boris Pasternak.* By Olga Hughes

*The Aesthetics of György Lukács.* By Béla Királyfalvi

*The Echoing Wood of Theodore Roethke.* By Jenijoy La Belle

*Achilles' Choice: Examples of Modern Tragedy.* By David Lenson

*The Figure of Faust in Valéry and Goethe.* By Kurt Weinberg

*The Situation of Poetry: Contemporary Poetry and Its Traditions.* By Robert Pinsky

*The Symbolic Imagination: Coleridge and the Romantic Tradition.* By J. Robert Barth, S. J.

*Adventures in the Deeps of the Mind: The Cuchulain Cycle of W. B. Yeats.* By Barton R. Friedman

*Shakespearean Representation: Mimesis and Modernity in Elizabethan Tragedy.* By Howard Felperin

*René Char: The Myth and the Poem.* By James R. Lawler

*Six French Poets of Our Time: A Critical and Historical Study.* By Robert W. Greene

*Coleridge's Metaphors of Being.* By Edward Kessler

*Library of Congress Cataloging in Publication Data*

Kessler, Edward, 1927-
  Coleridge's metaphors of being.

  (Princeton essays in literature)
  Includes index.
  1. Coleridge, Samuel Taylor, 1772-1834—Criticism and interpretation.  I. Title.
PR4484.K4      821'.7      78-70302
ISBN 0-691-06394-X